COLLINS GEM

CHEMISTRY
BASIC FACTS

W A H Scott BSc PhD

KU-051-586

HarperCollins*Publishers*

HarperCollins Publishers
PO Box, Glasgow G4 0NB, Scotland

First published 1982
Revised edition 1988
Third edition 1991

Reprint 10 9 8 7 6 5 4 3 2

© HarperCollins Publishers 1991

ISBN 0 00 470175 5

Printed in Great Britain by
HarperCollins Manufacturing, Glasgow

Introduction

Collins Gem *Basic Facts* is a series of illustrated GEM dictionaries in important school subjects. This new edition has been extensively revised and updated to widen the coverage of the subject and to reflect recent changes in the way it is taught in the classroom.

Bold words in an entry identify key terms which are explained in greater detail in entries of their own; important terms which do not have separate entries are shown in *italic* and are explained in the entry in which they occur.

Elements are presented in this consistent format:

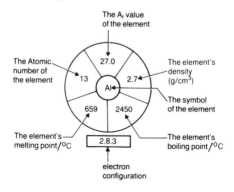

Other titles in the series include:

Gem *Basic Facts Mathematics*
Gem *Basic Facts Physics*
Gem *Basic Facts Biology*
Gem *Basic Facts Science*
Gem *Basic Facts Computing*
Gem *Basic Facts History*
Gem *Basic Facts Geography*
Gem *Basic Facts Craft, Design & Technology*
Gem *Basic Facts Business Studies*

A$_r$ The symbol for **relative atomic mass**. The A$_r$ value for an **element** is a measure of the **mass** of an average atom of the element compared to the mass of an atom of the **isotope** carbon-12. See **M$_r$**, **atomic mass**.

abrasive A hard material used to wear away or break up softer materials. Examples are **diamond**, silicon carbide (SiC), boron nitride (BN), and aluminium oxide (Al$_2$O$_3$).

absolute temperature See **Kelvin temperature scale**.

abundance A measure of how much of a substance exists; for example, of **elements** in a planet or of **isotopes** in an element. It is often expressed as a percentage.

Earth elements	O	Si	Al	Fe	Ca	Na	K	Mg
% abundance	46.6	27.7	8.1	5.0	3.6	2.8	2.6	2.1

(a)

Sun elements	H	He	O	C	Si
% abundance	54.0	44.7	0.8	0.4	0.05

(b)

Element	Isotope	% abundance
Chlorine	$^{35}_{17}Cl$	75.5
	$^{37}_{17}Cl$	24.5
Carbon	$^{12}_{6}C$	98.9
	$^{13}_{6}C$	1.1
Magnesium	$^{24}_{12}Mg$	78.6
	$^{25}_{12}Mg$	10.1
	$^{26}_{12}Mg$	11.3

(c)

abundance The abundance of (a) elements in the earth, (b) elements in the sun and (c) isotopes in some commonly occurring elements.

Knowing the percentage abundance of each isotope it is possible to calculate the A_r value for the element, e.g.:

$$^{35}_{17}Cl:^{37}_{17}Cl = 3:1$$

$$A_r(Cl) = \frac{(3 \times 35) + (1 \times 37)}{4} = 35.5$$

accelerator A chemical used to speed up **cross-linking** reactions in **polymers** or the **curing** of **epoxy resins**. See **catalyst**.

accumulator A rechargeable **battery**. The most common type is the lead-acid accumulator. This is the battery which is used to start cars and lorries. It is also used to drive milk floats and fork-lift trucks. In the future we shall probably drive electric cars which are powered by accumulators.

In the lead-acid accumulator the **electrolyte** is dilute **sulphuric acid**. The positive plate is made of lead(IV) oxide and the negative plate is composed of **lead**. When the accumulator is discharged (flat) the plates are coated with lead(II) sulphate. The sulphate coating is removed when the accumulator is recharged by passing electricity through it. The lead-acid accumulator is dangerous because it can produce very high currents. It produces the flammable gas **hydrogen** whilst it is being recharged and there is the constant danger of the **acid** spilling from the accumulator.

Another type is the **nickel**-cadmium accumulator. The positive plate is made of a complex nickel salt (nickel oxyhydroxide), while the negative plate is made up of cadmium. The electrolyte is potassium hydroxide solution which is soaked into a spongy material and so cannot spill. Because of this, this type of accumulator is termed 'dry'. Nickel-cadmium accumulators work well at low temperatures but, as yet, are very expensive.

acetic acid See **ethanoic acid**.

acid A substance which releases **hydrogen**

ions (H^+) when it is added to **water**. The hydrogen ion is *solvated*, that is, a water **molecule** adds on to it, to give the **oxonium ion** (H_3O^+). Acidic solutions have a **pH** of less than 7. Common laboratory acids are:

(a) **Nitric acid** (HNO_3).
(b) **Hydrochloric acid** (HCl).
(c) **Sulphuric acid** (H_2SO_4).
(d) **Ethanoic acid** (CH_3COOH).

These acids are dangerous, corrosive liquids and should always be treated with care.

Acids have the following properties:

(a) They turn blue **litmus** red.
(b) They give **carbon dioxide** when added to **carbonates**.
(c) They give **hydrogen** when added to certain metals.
(d) They neutralize **alkalis**.

acid-base reaction A reaction between an **acid** and a **base** to form a **salt** and **water** only. Some examples are shown here.

Hydrochloric acid HCl(aq)	+	Sodium hydroxide NaOH(aq)	$\rightarrow$	Sodium chloride NaCl(aq)	+	water H_2O(l)

Nitric acid $2HNO_3$(aq)	+	Copper(II) oxide CuO(s)	$\rightarrow$	Copper(II) nitrate $Cu(NO_3)_2$(aq)	+	water H_2O(l)

acid rain Rain polluted by a build-up of **acids** in the atmosphere. Rain is naturally acidic because of the **carbon dioxide** which is dissolved in it. However, **hydrogen chloride** and **sulphur dioxide** produced by industrial and some natural activities (e.g. earthquakes) combine with oxygen and water vapour in the **atmosphere** to produce strong acid **solutions**. These make the rain more acid which causes much damage to trees, lakes and buildings. The normal **pH** of rain is 5.6. The lowest pH of rain recorded in the UK is 2.4 which is over 1000 times more acidic. See **acidification**, **pollution**.

acid salts Salts in which only some of the replaceable **hydrogen atoms** in an **acid molecule** have been replaced by a metal. Some examples are shown below:

Na_2CO_3	Sodium carbonate	$NaHCO_3$	Sodium hydrogencarbonate
Na_2SO_4	Sodium sulphate	$NaHSO_4$	Sodium hydrogensulphate
Na_3PO_4	Sodium phosphate	Na_2HPO_4	Sodium hydrogenphosphate

acidic oxides Oxides of **non-metals** that react with water to form acidic **solutions**. Examples are given in the table overleaf.

Oxide		Acid	
Carbon dioxide	CO_2	Carbonic acid	H_2CO_3
Sulphur dioxide	SO_2	Sulphurous acid	H_2SO_3
Sulphur trioxide	SO_3	Sulphuric acid	H_2SO_4

acidic oxides   Examples of acids and the oxides from which they derive.

acidification   The fall in **pH** of water in lakes, rivers, wells and in the ground, caused by pollutants such as **sulphur dioxide** (SO_2) and **nitrogen oxides** (NO and N_2O and NO_2). These pollutants are produced in power stations, industry, the home, and internal combustion engines. They rise up into the **atmosphere** where they react to form acids which can be carried thousands of miles before falling to the ground, as **acid rain**, causing serious **pollution**. Animal and plant life are affected, as are buildings made of stone.

activation energy (E_a)   The energy needed to start off a reaction. When **hydrogen** and **oxygen** are mixed there is no **reaction**. When a **flame** is brought into contact with the gases, there is an immediate **explosion**. The heat of the flame causes the reaction to occur. Many chemical reactions are like this. It seems that there is a barrier which has to be overcome before the reaction will take place. **Energy**, as in the heat of the flame, has to be put in to make the reaction occur. See **catalyst**.

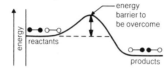

activation energy The energy barrier that has to be overcome for a reaction to take place.

active carbon Particles of **carbon** (**charcoal**) with a large surface area which can adsorb **molecules** onto their surfaces. Active carbon is used to purify **gases** and **liquids** and is widely employed today in **water** purification and the production of white **sugar**.

addition reaction A reaction in which two or more molecules are reacted together to form a single **molecule**. Good examples are found in the reactions of **alkenes** (see p. 8). These compounds contain **double bonds** and can add an **atom** to each side of the double bond to form a **saturated alkane**. Addition reactions also occur in the making of many **polymers**, e.g. **poly(ethene)**.

additive A small amount of substance added to a material to give it particular properties. They

addition reaction Ethene reacting with hydrogen.

are widely used today. Examples are:
(a) Anti-foaming agents in washing powders.
(b) Colouring materials in food and soft drinks.
(c) **Emulsifiers** in margarines.

adhesive A substance used to stick one material to another. Examples are glues, plant resins and **epoxy resins**. Adhesives are **polymers**. Some are already dissolved in a solvent which, when used, evaporates and leaves the adhesive behind to hold materials together. Others comes as two components, the **monomer** and an **initiator**, which have to be mixed when needed. Mixing produces the polymer which forms a strong **bond**.

aerosol Very small solid particles suspended in air. A natural example is smoke. The word is most commonly used, however, to describe the device which is used to create aerosols, the **aerosol can**.

aerosol can   A device for providing small amounts of chemicals in a finely-divided form. Aerosol cans have been used to deliver antiperspirants, shaving **foams**, paint, lubricants, ointments and foods such as cream. Because of the concern over **CFC** gases, the propellant used to push the contents out of the can is now usually an **alkane** such as butane. This is normally liquified under pressure and mixes with the material which is to be delivered. See **aerosol**.

aggregate   Any material which can be cemented together to form a **solid** material. Aggregates are used in road building, foundations of buildings and in producing building materials such as bricks, breeze blocks and **concrete**.

agrochemicals   Natural and synthetic chemicals used in the agriculture industry. Examples

Type	% use
Herbicide	40
Insecticide	30
Fungicide	20
Other	10

agrochemicals   The frequency of use of common agrochemicals.

include **biocides**, growth regulators, soil conditioners, and **vitamin** and **mineral** supplements. Note that **fertilizers** are not included in this definition.

air The **mixture** of gases which surrounds the earth. The average composition of pure air is shown below. This composition varies from place to place and also varies with altitude. See **Earth's atmosphere**.

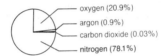

oxygen (20.9%)
argon (0.9%)
carbon dioxide (0.03%)
nitrogen (78.1%)

Other components
neon, helium, krypton, xenon — In small constant amounts.
water — In very variable amounts.

air The composition of air.

Air also contains pollutants, some of which are shown below.

Pollutant	Sources
Sulphur dioxide	Burning coal, oil
Carbon monoxide	Engines, cigarettes
Oxides of nitrogen	Car engines
Soot	Fires, engines
Pollen	Trees, flowers
Dust	Volcanoes

Air is vital for life. The **oxygen** is necessary for **respiration** and the **carbon dioxide** is needed for **photosynthesis**.

alcohols Alcohols are important **organic compounds**. They possess the arrangement of atoms:

$$\begin{array}{c} \diagdown \qquad\quad \text{H} \\ -\text{C}-\text{O}\diagup \\ \diagup \end{array}$$

The −OH group is the **functional group** of the alcohols. **Ethanol** is the most important compound but see also **methanol** and **glycol**.

Alcohols with a small M_r value are flammable liquids which dissolve in water. Some of the important properties of alcohols are that they can be oxidized easily, they form **esters** and react with **sodium** to produce **hydrogen**.

alkali A **base** which is soluble in water. Alkalis are usually metal **hydroxides**, e.g. **sodium hydroxide**, but **ammonia solution** is also an alkali. Their reactions are affected by their **strength** and their **concentration**.

Oven cleaners, household **ammonia** and some paint strippers contain alkalis. Alkalis have the following properties:

(a) They turn red **litmus** blue.

(b) They neutralize **acids**.

(c) They have a **pH** above 7.

(d) They react with acids to produce a **salt** and **water** only.

alkali metals Very reactive **metals** found in **group** I of the **periodic table**. These **metals** react with water to form **solutions** which are **alkaline**. For example:

$$2Na(s) + 2H_2O(l) \rightarrow 2NaOH(aq) + H_2(g)$$

alkaline Used to describe a **solution** whose **pH** is greater than 7. See **alkali**, **alkali metals**, **alkaline earth metal**.

alkaline earth metal A metal found in **group** II of the **periodic table**. Such metals are less reactive than the **alkali metals** found in group I, but, like them, produce **alkaline** solutions when reacted with **water**.

alkanes Important **hydrocarbon** compounds in our lives. Our **gas** supplies (North Sea gas and 'Calor' gas) are almost 100% alkanes. Vaseline or petroleum jelly is made of alkanes. The chief source of alkanes is **petroleum** and they are valuable **raw materials** in the chemical industry. They have a **general formula**: C_nH_{2n+2} so the alkane with 4 **carbon** atoms will have 10 **hydrogen** atoms: C_4H_{10}, **butane**.

They are **saturated** compounds and so are not very reactive. They tend to be **flammable** and will react with **chlorine** in the presence of **ultra-violet radiation**. See also **methane, ethane** and **propane**.

alkenes   Important **hydrocarbon** compounds. They are widely made in oil refineries and are used as starting materials in the manufacture of many materials, e.g. **plastics**. **Ethene, propene** and styrene (phenylethene) are three of the most important alkenes.

  They have a **general formula**: C_nH_{2n}. So the alkene with 3 carbon atoms (propene) will have 6 hydrogen atoms. Because they are **unsaturated compounds** they have a carbon–carbon **double bond** and are reactive compounds. Typically they will undergo **addition reactions** with **hydrogen, halogens** and **water**. They will also form **polymers** by this addition process. See **poly(phenylethene)** and **poly(propene)**.

alkynes   There is only one common alkyne. This is **ethyne**. Alkynes have the **general formula** C_nH_{2n-2} and so, ethyne with 2 carbon atoms will have 2 hydrogen atoms: C_2H_2. Alkynes have carbon–carbon **triple bonds** and therefore show the typical **addition reactions** of **unsaturated compounds**.

allotropes   Elements which exist in different forms in the same physical state. The chemical **properties** are the same but the physical properties are different. The best example is **carbon**. There are two allotropes: **diamond** and **graphite**. Diamond is hard and colourless, graphite is flakey and black. Other elements which exist in different allotropic forms are **sulphur**, **phosphorus** and **tin**.

alloy A **mixture** which is made up of two or more **metals** or which contains metals and **non-metals**.

Alloys are much more widely used than **pure** metals because, by bringing two or more **elements** together in the right proportions, specific properties can be obtained. For example, **aluminium** is quite a soft metal but when a small amount of **copper** is mixed in, the alloy duralumin is produced which is strong enough to be used in aircraft frames. Some common examples are: **brass**, **bronze**, **duralumin**, **pewter**, **solder** and **steel**.

alpha particles ($_2^4He^{2+}$) **Helium atoms** without their electrons. They are produced in many **nuclear reactions**. They have a fairly short range in **air** (usually less than 10 cm) and are easily stopped by thin sheets of **paper** or foil.

alumina Another name for aluminium oxide (Al_2O_3). It is the chief constituent of **bauxite** from which **aluminium** is produced. Alumina itself is useful as a **refractory material** and as a support material for **catalysts**.

aluminium The most abundant **metal** in the earth's crust (approximately 8% by **mass**). **Clay**, shale, slate and **granite** all contain aluminium compounds but the metal is difficult to extract from them. It is obtained by the **electrolysis** of **bauxite** dissolved in **cryolite**, using graphite electrodes.

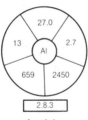

aluminium

The metal has **valency** of 3. Although it is very reactive, this metal and its alloys are resistant to **corrosion** because of a layer of **oxide** on the surface of the metal. It is subject to anodizing (see **anodize**).

Aluminium metal is **malleable**, easy to handle, has a low density and its **alloys** can be very strong. The metal and alloys are used in a great many ways. Examples include:

(a) Construction, in window and door frames;
(b) Transport, in car bodies, engines, aeroplanes, cycle frames, ship superstructures;
(c) Electricity, in power lines;
(d) Food, in milk bottle tops and baking foil.

aluminium compounds

Aluminium chloride $AlCl_3$	The **anhydrous** chloride is **covalent**.
Aluminium oxide Al_2O_3	The oxide is **amphoteric**.
Aluminium sulphate $Al_2(SO_4)_3$	The most important aluminium compound. It is used as a precipitator in sewage works, as a mordant and as a size in the paper industry. It is also used as a foaming agent in fire-extinguishers.

amalgam   An **alloy** which contains **mercury**. **Zinc** amalgam is used for teeth fillings. *Amalgamation*, the process of forming an amalgam, was once used to extract **gold** and **silver** from crushed rock which contained the metals.

amino acids   These are **organic compounds** which contain $-COOH$ and $-NH_2$ groups. They are the building bricks from which **proteins** are made. Twenty different amino acids are needed to make up all the proteins in our bodies. Our bodies can produce some of these amino acids but we need to take in eight particular ones through eating. These are known as *essential* amino acids. Amino acids combine together to form **peptides**.

amino acids Glycine, the simplest of the amino acids.

ammonia (NH₃) A colourless **gas** with a pungent odour. It is very **soluble** in **water** giving an **alkaline** solution. Ammonia was once made from **coal** but now over 90% comes from the **Haber process**.

Ammonia is also produced by bacteria found on the roots of leguminous plants (peas and beans). When protein decomposes, ammonia is released. Both of these are important sources of plant food. See the **nitrogen cycle**. The importance of ammonia in our lives is shown in the diagram.

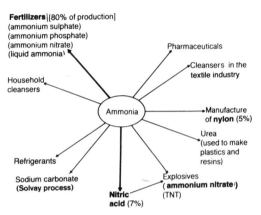

ammonia   The uses of ammonia.

Ammonia is a **covalent compound**. It has a characteristic reaction with **hydrogen chloride** to give dense white fumes of ammonium chloride:

$$NH_3(g) + HCl(g) \rightarrow NH_4Cl(s)$$

Ammonia can be oxidized to **nitric acid** and this is the major source of nitric acid today. It is easily liquefied and it is usually carried in this state from place to place in tankers.

ammonia solution (NH₄OH) (formerly called **ammonium hydroxide**) A solution of **ammonia** in **water**.

ammonium compounds

Ammonium carbonate $(NH_4)_2CO_3$	An unstable compound used as smelling salts (*sal volatile*).
Ammonium chloride NH_4Cl	A salt which undergoes **dissociation** into ammonia and hydrogen chloride.
Ammonium nitrate NH_4NO_3	A very important compound which is used as a **fertilizer** and an explosive.
Ammonium phosphate $(NH_4)_3PO_4$	A convenient chemical with which to put both nitrogen and phosphorus into the soil.
Ammonium sulphate $(NH_4)_2SO_4$	An important fertilizer.

ammonium ion Found in ammonium compounds as well as in a **solution** of ammonia gas in **water**. The ion is positively charged and the **hydrogen** atoms are arranged around the **nitrogen** atom in a **tetrahedral** way.

$NH_4{}^+$

amphoteric Describes insoluble **oxides** and **hydroxides** which show both basic and acidic **properties**. The examples shown here will react with both **acids** and **alkalis** to form **salts**:

Al_2O_3	PbO	ZnO
$Al(OH)_3$	$Pb(OH)_2$	$Zn(OH)_2$

For example:

$$ZnO + 2HCl \rightarrow ZnCl_2 + 2H_2O$$
$$ZnO + 2NaOH + H_2O \rightarrow Na_2Zn(OH)_4$$
$$\text{(sodium zincate)}$$

amorphous Without definite shape or form. Material which is non-crystalline, that is appears to have no regularity of shape, is described as amorphous.

ampère (amp) The **unit** of electric current. Its shortened form is *amp* and its symbol A. It measures the rate of flow of charge. $1\,A = 1$ **coulomb/second**. See **SI units**.

anaesthetic A substance which reduces or removes the feeling of pain. General anaesthetics, such as diethyl ether or nitrous oxide, produce unconsciousness. Local anaesthetics only affect a small part of the body while the person stays awake. See **ethers**, **nitrogen oxides**.

analysis A process to find out what a material

is made up of. **Qualitative** analysis provides information about what the material contains; for example, which elements are present in a compound or which compounds are found in a **mixture**. **Quantitative** analysis provides information about how much of particular substances there is; for example, the percentage composition of a food in terms of **fat**, **protein** and **carbohydrate**, or the amount of **alcohol** in a person's blood.

anhydrides Substances which react with **water** to produce **acids**. All **acidic oxides** are anhydrides, but some will give rise to one acid only whilst others will produce two. For example:
(a) SO_3 gives rise to H_2SO_4.
(b) NO_2 gives rise to HNO_3 and HNO_2.

anhydrite The **mineral** calcium sulphate ($CaSO_4$). It is widely used in the manufacture of **sulphuric acid**.

anhydrous Containing no **water**. The term usually denotes **salts** with no **water of crystallization**. For example:

> anhydrous copper(II) sulphate $CuSO_4$
> anhydrous sodium carbonate Na_2CO_3

The **hydrated** salts are:

> $CuSO_4.5H_2O$
> $Na_2CO_3.10H_2O$

The term is also used about liquids which are perfectly dry, e.g. anhydrous **ether**.

anion A negatively charged **ion**. Anions usually contain a full outer orbital of **electrons**. **Non-metals** form anions but complex ions can also be anions. For example:

Sulphate SO_4^{2-} Manganate(VII) MnO_4^-
Carbonate CO_3^{2-} Nitrate NO_3^-

annealing A method of strengthening a material by heating and controlled cooling. Heating and cooling **metals** causes changes in their **properties**, especially their strength. When a metal is heated to a high **temperature** and then cooled slowly the **crystals** grow very large. The metal then becomes **malleable**.

The continuous annealing process now used in the production of **tinplate** is much more rapid than the previous batch process. What used to take many hours, now takes only a few minutes.

anode The **electrode** which carries the positive charge in a solution that has undergone **electrolysis**. **Anions** are attracted to the anode because they are negatively charged. The **ions** give up their extra **electrons** at the anode. Non-metallic **elements** are produced and the electrons travel round the circuit. See **cathode**.

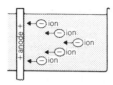

anode Negatively charged ions attracted to the positive anode.

anodize To coat a metal with a protective oxide film. For example, **aluminium** has a protective layer of **oxide** (Al_2O_3). This layer of oxide can be thickened by making the piece of aluminium the **anode** (+) in an **electrolysis cell**. Dilute **sulphuric acid** is used as the **electrolyte**. Aluminium atoms give up **electrons** and they react with the **water**:

$$2Al(s) + 3H_2O(l) \rightarrow$$
$$Al_2O_3(s) + 6H^+(aq) + 6 \text{ electrons}^-.$$

Aluminium oxide is formed and this can be dyed to produce attractive finishes to products, e.g. coloured milk-bottle tops.

antacids Substances used to reduce the **pH** of stomach juices and, therefore, relieve indigestion. Sodium hydrogencarbonate ($NaHCO_3$) and magnesium oxide (MgO) are common examples.

anti-foaming agents **Additives** used in washing powders, **paper** manufacture and many other industrial processes. The amount of **foam** is reduced and the process becomes more efficient.

antifreeze A substance which is added to the cooling system of engines in winter to prevent the formation of **ice** which would damage the engine. The substances added lower the freezing point of the **water**. Examples are methanol and ethane-1,2-diol.

anti-knock See **octane rating**.

antioxidants Chemical **additives** which slow down oxidation reactions. They are widely used in manufactured foods, particularly those containing fat. They increase the *shelf-life* of the food, that is, the amount of time it can be kept before being eaten. Many antioxidants used in food are natural substances.

Antioxidants, usually in the form of **aromatic** compounds, are also added to a wide number of **rubber** and **plastic** materials.

amu (atomic mass unit) A simple and convenient way of comparing the **masses** of atomic particles (**nucleons**) and **isotopes** which avoids using very small numbers. The **proton** and the **neutron** are each given the value of 1 amu.

aq Abbreviation used to denote an **aqueous solution**, e.g. NaCl(aq).

aqueous solution A solution where **water** is the **solvent**.

argon (Ar) The most abundant **noble gas**. It makes up 0.9% of the **atmosphere** (by **volume**). It is very unreactive. No **compound** of argon has yet been made.

Argon has uses where the presence of an unreactive gas is needed. 90% of argon production is used in arc welding and in metal manufacture, melting and casting; 10% is used, mixed with a small amount of **nitrogen**, in electric light bulbs and fluorescent tubes.

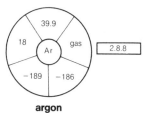

argon

aromatic Describes compounds containing a **benzene** ring **structure** in their **molecules**.

arsenic A brittle grey **metalloid**. Its **compounds** are very poisonous — especially the oxide (As_2O_3). It is a group v element which occurs as **allotropes**. Arsenic compounds are used in pesticides. The grey allotrope **sublimes** at 613 °C.

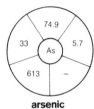

arsenic

asbestos A naturally occurring silicate which was widely used in the past for fireproof clothing and insulating materials. Its use today is restricted because of the dangers of contracting *asbestosis*, a fatal lung disease. It was much used in schools as bench mats and centre pieces for gauzes. These are now made of material which does not contain asbestos.

asphalt A mixture of **bitumen** and **aggregate** used widely in the surfacing of roads.

atmosphere 1. A unit of **pessure**. Although the pressure of the air which surrounds us varies from place to place and from time to time its value usually only varies slightly and is always approximately one atmosphere.

2. The mixture of gases which surrounds a planet, sun or moon. See **Earth's atmosphere**.

atom The smallest indivisible particle of an **element** that can exist, the building bricks with which everything is made. An atom can be thought of as the smallest part of an element that can take part in a chemical **reaction**. They are small particles; 100 million placed end-to-end would measure 1 cm. They are made up of even smaller **subatomic particles**:

(a) **Neutrons (n)** and **protons (p)** are particles found in the centre of the atom — the **nucleus**.

(b) **Electrons (e)** are particles that move round the nucleus.

The atom as a whole is electrically **neutral** although the protons and electrons carry electrical charges. These charges are equal in size but opposite in sign, hence the number of protons always equals the number of electrons. Atoms which lose or gain electrons are called **ions**. All atoms of the same **element** contain the same number of protons and have the same **atomic number**, but atoms of the same element can contain different numbers of neutrons. See **isotope**.

atomic mass Atoms have different masses if they contain different numbers of **protons**, **neutrons** and **electrons**. Because these particles are so small the mass of an atom is tiny.

It is not usual to refer to the mass of an atom in grammes or kilogrammes so we normally compare the mass of one atom with a standard mass. This is called the **relative atomic mass** (A_r).

atomic number (Z)   The number of **protons** in the **nucleus** of an **atom**. All atoms of the same **element** have the same atomic number, e.g. **sodium** atoms all contain 11 protons. In a **neutral** atom the number of **electrons** equals the atomic number.

atomicity   The number of **atoms** in a **molecule** of an **element**. With the **noble gases** there is only one atom in the molecule and the atomocity is 1. All other gases have an atomicity of 2, e.g. **oxygen** (O_2), **nitrogen** (N_2), except **ozone** (O_3). Molecules in solid **sulphur** have an atomicity of 8 (S_8).

Avogadro constant/number (L)   The number of **atoms** that are contained in exactly 12 g of the carbon-12 **isotope**. More generally it is the number of particles present in a **mole** of substance. $L = 6 \times 10^{23} \text{ mol}^{-1}$.

   Named after the Italian physicist Amedeo Avogadro, 1776–1836, famous for his work on gases.

Avogadro's hypothesis/law   A hypothesis that states that under the same conditions of

temperature and **pressure**, equal **volumes** of gases contain the same number of **molecules**, e.g. 10 **dm**^{3} of oxygen and 10 dm^3 of hydrogen both contain the same number of molecules. They contain twice as many molecules as 5 dm^3 of **chlorine**, provided all the volumes were measured at the same temperature and pressure.

bakelite See **phenol/methanal resins**.

baking powder A mixture of a **carbonate** and a weak **acid** which is used in cooking. When **water** is added to the **solid** mixture or the **mixture** is heated, **carbon dioxide** is produced. This produces bubbles in the dough or cake mixture and it rises, producing a product with an open texture. The mixture usually contains **sodium hydrogencarbonate** ($NaHCO_3$) and tartaric

The powder can be made up in the kitchen by mixing cream of tartar (the **potassium** salt of tartaric acid) and baking soda (sodium hydrogencarbonate). This prevents the **reaction** from occurring before it is required.

balance 1. A device for comparing the **masses** of objects. It is usual to use digital electric balances in schools these days.

2. Chemical **equations** must be 'balanced'. It is necessary to have equal numbers of each atom on each side of the equation as atoms can neither be created nor destroyed. For example:

Zn(s) + HCl(aq) → ZnCl₂(aq) + H₂(g)

No. of atoms:

$Zn = 1$ $H = 1$ $Cl = 1$ $Zn = 1$ $Cl = 2$ $H = 2$

The equation *is not* balanced.

Zn(s) + 2HCl(aq) → ZnCl₂(aq) + H₂(g)

The equation *is* balanced.

barium   A very reactive **group** II **element**. It occurs in nature as the **sulphate** (**barytes**) and as the **carbonate**. The **metal** is extracted from the molten **chloride** by **electrolysis**. Barium chloride **solution** is used to test for sulphates.

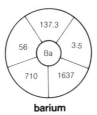

barium

barrel   **1.** A cask for holding beer. It has a **volume** of exactly 32 imperial gallons.
2. A unit volume in the **petroleum** industry. One barrel=approximately 35 imperial gallons (159 litres).

barytes   A common barium sulphate ($BaSO_4$) **mineral** used as a source of **barium** compounds.

base   A substance which reacts with an acid to form a **salt** and **water** only. Bases are usually **metal oxides** or **hydroxides**, e.g. sodium hydroxide (NaOH) and copper(II) oxide (CuO).

$$NaOH(aq) + HCl(aq) \rightarrow NaCl(aq) + H_2O(l)$$
$$CuO(s) + H_2SO_4(aq) \rightarrow CuSO_4(aq) + H_2O(l)$$

Metal oxides and hydroxides which are soluble in water are known as **alkalis**. These are compounds of **group** I and II metals.

Ammonia solution is an alkali. It contains **hydroxide ions** in **equilibrium**.

$$NH_3(g) + H_2O(l) \rightleftharpoons NH_4^+(aq) + OH^-(aq)$$

basic oxide   An oxide which reacts with an **acid** to form a **salt** and **water** only. Basic oxides are oxides of **metals**, but not all metals give basic oxides. See **amphoteric**, **acidic oxide**.

basic   oxygen   process   See   **steel manufacture**.

basic salts   Salts which contain **hydroxide ions** as well as normal **anions**, e.g. **sulphate**, **carbonate**. Common examples are:

Malachite	$CuCO_3 . Cu(OH)_2$
Azurite	$2CuCO_3 . Cu(OH)_2$
White lead	$2PbCO_3 . Pb(OH)_2$

battery A device which converts chemical **energy** into electrical energy. Chemical **reactions** occur and, in them, **electrons** are sent through a circuit. Batteries are of two types: the rechargeable, also known as **accumulators**, and the non-rechargeable.

Batteries are available in different shapes, sizes and price ranges and their chemical composition varies too. The common 'dry battery' (the Leclanché dry cell) has **carbon** and **zinc electrodes**, and a **gel** of ammonium chloride as the **electrolyte**. It produces a voltage of 1.5 volts. See **cell**.

bauxite The chief **ore** from which **aluminium** is extracted. It is a **hydrated** oxide ($Al_2O_3 . xH_2O$) and is found in tropical regions of the world, e.g. Northern Australia and West Africa.

Benedict's solution A **solution** which can be used as a test for a **reducing agent**. It consists of a mixture of copper(II) sulphate, sodium carbonate and sodium citrate dissolved in water. A brown/red/yellow colour is formed when a **reducing agent** is warmed with the solution. It is most often used to test for reducing **sugars**, such as **glucose**.

benzene (C_6H_6) The simplest **aromatic compound**. It is a toxic liquid **hydrocarbon** which can cause cancers. Its widespread use in schools has been replaced by that of **methylbenzene**. It is produced from **naphtha**, and is an important source of **organic** compounds which are used to produce **poly(phenylethene)**, **phenol**, **detergents** and **nylon**.

benzene

beta particles These are **electrons** which are produced in the following **nuclear reaction**:

$$\underset{\text{neutron}}{_{0}^{1}\text{n}} \rightarrow \underset{\text{proton}}{_{1}^{1}\text{p}} + \underset{\text{electron}}{_{-1}^{0}\text{e}}$$

For example,

$$_{15}^{31}\text{P} + _{0}^{1}\text{n} \rightarrow _{15}^{32}\text{P} \rightarrow _{16}^{32}\text{S} + _{-1}^{0}\text{e}$$

In this **radioactive** decay the electrons are expelled from the **nucleus** of the **atom**. They travel at high speeds (up to 98% of the speed of light) and have a greater penetrating power than **alpha particles**. When this reaction occurs, the atom concerned changes its **atomic number** because it gains a **proton**.

biocide A chemical which is used to kill or control living organisms. Biocides used on plants are known as herbicides; those used on fungi are called fungicides, and those used on animals are known as pesticides.

biodegradable Used to describe any material which can be broken down by micro-organisms in the soil. Some packaging material now has **starch** incorporated into the **plastic** structure so that it can be broken down.

biomass Any plant material which might be used as a resource. Examples are trees, grass, waste vegetables, sewage, farm slurries. Biomass can be used as a direct source of **energy** (e.g. by burning wood or straw), can be decomposed to produce fuels (e.g. by **fermentation** of waste to make **methane**) or as a feedstock for the chemical industry.

bitumen A mixture of **hydrocarbons** of a high **boiling-point** which is left behind in the **distillation** of **petroleum**. It is used for roofing and road surfacing. See **asphalt**.

blast furnace A furnace allowing a continuous production of molten **iron**. At the bottom of the furnace the **coke** and hot **air** react:

$$C(s) + O_2(g) \rightarrow CO_2(g)$$

This **exothermic** reaction raises the **temperature** to 1800°C. The coke then reacts with the **carbon dioxide**:

$$C(s) + CO_2(g) \rightarrow 2CO(g)$$

The carbon monoxide formed reduces the iron **oxides** to iron (1200°C). For example:

$$Fe_2O_3(s) + 3CO(g) \rightarrow 3CO_2(g) + 2Fe(l)$$

The moltern iron flows to the bottom of the furnace. The **limestone** in the charge is

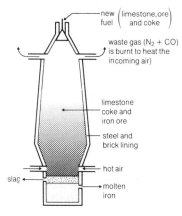

new fuel (limestone, ore and coke)

waste gas (N_2 + CO) is burnt to heat the incoming air)

limestone coke and iron ore

steel and brick lining

hot air

slag

molten iron

blast furnace

decomposed by the heat producing calcium oxide and carbon dioxide.

The calcium oxide reacts with impurities from the iron ore (mainly silica (SiO_2)) and forms a molten slag:

$$CaO(s) + SiO_2(s) \rightarrow CaSiO_3(l)$$

This sinks to the bottom of the furnace where it floats on top of the iron. The iron which is produced contains about 3% **carbon** and the **metal** is brittle. In **steel manufacture** the amount of impurities in the iron is very carefully controlled.

bleach A substance used to decolourize materials, e.g. fabrics and **paper**. Sunlight and **oxygen** act as bleaches but the most commonly found bleach is sodium chlorate(I) **solution** (NaClO). This is produced when **chlorine** is reacted with **sodium hydroxide** solution:

$$Cl_2(g) + 2NaOH(aq) \rightarrow$$
$$NaCl(aq) + NaClO(aq) + H_2O(l)$$

Domestic bleaches such as 'Domestos' contain sodium chlorate(I) solution. The chlorate(I) decomposes to give oxygen which acts as an **oxidizing agent**:

$$NaClO + coloured \rightarrow NaCl + oxidized$$
$$material \qquad\qquad (decolourized)$$
$$material$$

bleaching powder A white powder of complex composition. It is made by the action of **chlorine** on calcium hydroxide. It contains calcium chlorate(I) $Ca(OCl)_2$. The powder releases **chlorine** when it is treated with dilute **acid**.

blockboard Material made from two sheets of **veneer** which are separated by a core made up of lengths of softwood. Blockboard is cheap but strong and is often used for doors.

boiling The change from the **liquid state** to the **gas** state at a fixed **temperature**: the **boiling point**. Boiling takes place when the **vapour** pressure of the liquid equals the **pressure** of the **atmosphere** above the liquid.

boiling point The **temperature** at which **boiling** occurs. It is not fixed. It depends on the atmospheric **pressure**. The higher the pressure, the higher the boiling point. Boiling temperatures are also affected by impurities in the **liquid**. The presence of impurities causes the boiling temperature to rise. See **evaporation**.

bonds The links holding together **atoms** in **molecules** and **giant structures**. These chemical bonds are the forces which exist between the atoms and are generated by **electrons**. Electrons are either *shared between* atoms, or atoms *gain* or *lose* electrons forming **ions**.

The sharing of electrons (**covalent bonding**) usually occurs when two non-metallic atoms join together, e.g. H—H or H—Cl. The loss or gain of electrons (**ionic** or **electrovalent bonding**) occurs when atoms of metallic elements join with those of non-metallic elements, e.g. Na + Cl or Mg + O.

the sharing of electrons
e.g. hydrogen (H_2)

$$Na - e^- \atop Cl + e^-\} \rightarrow$$

the loss and gain of electrons e.g. sodium chloride (Na Cl)

bonds

boron A non-metallic **element** (see **non-metal**) in **group** III of the **periodic table**. Its

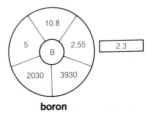

boron

oxide is used to make **glass** (see **borosilicate glass**). It is a component of **alloys** and is a moderator in nuclear reactors. See **nuclear reactions**.

borosilicate glass **Glass** made by the addition of **boron** oxide (B_2O_3) during its manufacture. This results in a material which does not expand very much. Consequently the glass can be heated or cooled rapidly without cracking. 'Pyrex' glassware is like this.

Boyle's law A law that states that at constant **temperature** the **volume** of a fixed **mass** of **gas**

$$P \propto \frac{1}{V}$$

$$P.V. = \text{constant}$$

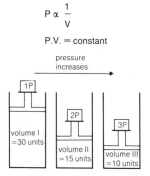

Boyle's law As the pressure doubles the volume is halved.

is inversely proportional to the **pressure** of the gas. In other words, if the pressure is *doubled* the volume is *halved*.

Named after the Irish scientist Robert Boyle, 1627–91, famous for his work on gases. See **Charles' law**, **gas laws**.

brass An **alloy** of **copper** and **zinc** which usually contains about 30% zinc. Brass is an attractive yellow-golden coloured material which is used for ornaments and for electrical components, e.g. in electrical plugs.

breath test A test used to measure the amount of **ethanol** drunk in alcoholic drinks by a person. A person blows into a machine which analyses the amount of ethanol in the breath. The machine converts this reading into a measure of the amount of ethanol in the blood. The current legal limit is 80 mg of ethanol per 100 ml of blood. Above this limit a driver is committing an offence in the UK.

brewing A process which involves the **fermentation** of **sugars** to the **alcohol**, **ethanol**. Beers, wines and spirits are produced by the brewing industry.

brine A **solution** of **sodium chloride** in **water**. The solution is more concentrated than seawater and is used in the food-processing industry, e.g. the production of bacon and in the preservation of many foods. In the chemical industry **chlorine** is produced by the **electrolysis** of brine. See **curing**.

bromide A **compound** of **bromine** and another **element**. **Metal** bromides are usually **ionic** solids, e.g. sodium bromide NaBr. See **halides**. **Non-metal** bromides are usually **covalent** compounds, e.g. hydrogen bromide HBr.

bromine (Br₂) A member of the **halogen** group of **elements**. It is a **volatile** red **liquid** at room **temperature**. The liquid is very **corrosive** and the vapour is both irritating and poisonous.

Although it is less reactive than **chlorine**, bromine will react vigorously with metals forming **bromides**:

$$Mg(s) + Br_2(l) \rightarrow MgBr_2(s)$$

bromine

Bromine is extracted from seawater by treatment with **chlorine** and sulphur dioxide. One thousand litres of seawater contains about 65 g of bromine.

% of production	Use
24	**Fuel additives**
20	Flame retardants
18	**Oil** well fluids
13	**Agrochemicals**
6	**Dyes**
4	Water purification
15	Other

bromine The uses of bromine in the mid-1980s.

Because of the increasing use of **unleaded petrol**, the amount of the fuel additive (1,2-dibromoethane) being added to **petrol** is now much less than it was. See **octane rating**.

bromine Chemical formula of the fuel additive 1,2-dibromoethane

bronze The combination of **copper** (>90%)

with **tin** (<10%) which results in an **alloy** which is much stronger than copper. The discovery of bronze in the Middle East (3000 BC) gave rise to important changes in the way humans lived (the Bronze Age). Nowadays, bronze is mainly used for gear wheels and engine bearings and, of course, as medals, e.g. for the Olympic Games.

Brownian motion Particles suspended in a **liquid** or **gas**, such as pollen in **water** or smoke in **air**, are seen to move in a random way. The explanation is that the microscopic particles which make up the liquid or gas, e.g. water and air **molecules**, are moving randomly and are hitting against the larger particles of pollen or smoke, causing them to move. Brownian motion is put forward as evidence for the **kinetic theory**.

Named after the Scottish botanist Robert Brown, 1773–1858, who was the first to observe the phenomenon.

burner (or Bunsen burner) A device invented in the 19th century so that coal-gas could be burnt cleanly giving a hot flame. **Natural gas** is now used. With the air hole open the **gas** is mixed with **air** and this makes sure that all the gas is burnt and no soot is produced. With the air hole shut a yellow sooty flame is produced because the gas is not fully burnt. See **flame**.

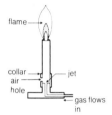

flame

collar
air
hole

jet

gas flows
in

burner The components of a Bunsen burner.

burning See **combustion**.

butane An **alkane** compound. It is a **gas** at **room temperature** but it is easily liquefied. It is present (dissolved) in **petroleum** and is used in refineries both as a **fuel** and as a starting material for the production of **hydogen** and **petrol** components. See **refining**.

It is a major component of '**Calor gas**'. The gas burns in **air**:

$$2C_4H_{10}(g) + 13O_2(g) \rightarrow 8CO_2(g) + 10H_2O(g)$$

by-product Something which is produced in a reaction in addition to the product which is required. For example, **slag** is a by-product of making **iron** in the **blast furnace** and **carbon dioxide** is a by-product of the **fermentation** pro-

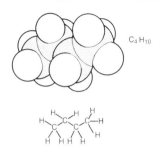

C_4H_{10}

butane   An alkane **compound**.

cess. It is important, if processes are to be economic, that by-products are sold, e.g. slag is sold as road-making material.

calcite   A **mineral** form of **calcium carbonate** ($CaCO_3$) which is found in **limestone** and **chalk**.

calcium   A soft, metallic **element** which is in **group** II of the **periodic table**. It is a fairly reactive **metal**, giving a slow but steady stream of **hydrogen** when it is added to cold water. 3.6% of the earth is made up of calcium **compounds**. Many of these are very common, e.g. **limestone** and **chalk** ($CaCO_3$). Calcium is obtained by the **electrolysis** of molten calcium chloride.

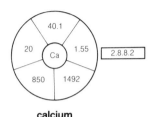

calcium

calcium compounds

Calcium carbonate $CaCO_3$	Used as building stone and in the production of **cement**. **Lime** (calcium oxide) is produced from calcium carbonate in a lime kiln. See **hardness of water**.
Calcium chloride $CaCl_2$	Used to produce calcium metal. The **anhydrous salt** is used as a drying agent.
Calcium hydrogen-carbonate $Ca(HCO_3)_2$	An important cause of temporary **hardness** in water.
Calcium hydroxide (slaked lime) $Ca(OH)_2$	A slightly soluble alkali. The aqueous solution is called **limewater**. It is used to make mortar.
Calcium oxide CaO	This is **lime**. It has very important uses in agriculture to combat excess acidity in soil.

Calcium sulphate $CaSO_4$	Gives rise to permanent hardness in water. It is found as **anhydrite** and **gypsum**.

calor gas A mixture of **hydrocarbon** compounds which is used as a portable supply of **gas**. It is made up of mainly **propane** (C_3H_8) and **butane** (C_4H_{10}) and these **compounds** are stored in metallic bottles under **pressure.**

cane sugar   See **sucrose.**

carbohydrate **Organic** compounds which contain the **elements, carbon, hydrogen** and **oxygen** only. Their formulae are always of the form: $C_x(H_2O)_y$, e.g. **sugars** such as **glucose** ($C_6H_{12}O_6$), **sucrose** ($C_{12}H_{22}O_{11}$) and ribose ($C_5H_{10}O_5$) and **polymers** such as **starch** ($C_6H_{10}O_5$)$_n$ and **cellulose** ($C_6H_{10}O_5$)$_n$. See **monosaccharide, disaccharide** and **polysaccharide.**

carbon A **non-metallic element** (see **nonmetal**) which is in **group** IV of the **periodic table.** It is found in nature as two **allotropes**: **diamond** and **graphite.**

All living tissue contains **carbon** compounds (**organic** compounds), e.g. **carbohydrates, proteins, fats,** and without these compounds life would be impossible.

Although the **element** burns in **oxygen** or **air** it is otherwise fairly unreactive. It is an important **reducing agent**. **Coke**, **coal** and **charcoal** are all impure forms of carbon. Carbon is also found combined in materials such as **limestone**, in the form of metal carbonates.

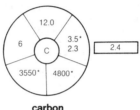

carbon

carbon compounds

Carbon dioxide CO_2

This **gas** can be formed by the action of heat or **acids** on **carbonates** or by the complete combustion of **carbon**. It is also produced in the **fermentation** of **sugars**. The test for carbon dioxide is that it turns **limewater** milky. Carbon dioxide plays a vital role in **photosynthesis** and the **carbon cycle**. See **greenhouse gases**.

Carbon monoxide CO

This gas is formed when carbon or its compounds are not completely burnt. It is an **air** pollutant, being produced in internal combustion engines and from the burning of cigarettes. It is a very poisonous gas because it combines with the **haemoglobin** in blood. It is useful as a **reducing agent** in the **blast furnace**. The gas burns to give **carbon dioxide**.

carbon cycle The process in which every time an animal or plant respires or a fuel is burnt **carbon dioxide** is released into the **atmosphere**. The cycle is carried on by the process of **photosynthesis** which continually takes carbon dioxide out of the **atmosphere** and builds up plant structures with it. In these processes carbon dioxide is cycled round the earth. There are

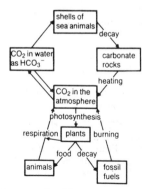

carbon cycle The processes which cycle carbon dioxide around the Earth.

stores of it (dissolved in the oceans, lakes and rivers) in **carbonate** rocks and in fossil **fuels**. A simple diagram of these movements is shown here. Some changes occur quickly, e.g. burning, others very slowly, e.g. formation of rocks.

carbon dating Method of telling the age of once-living material. **Carbon** has a **radioactive** isotope ($^{14}_{6}C$) and the atmospheric **carbon dioxide** contains a small constant proportion of this **isotope**. All carbon **compounds** in living tissue contain this carbon-14 isotope in the same constant proportion. When an animal or plant dies, however, the proportion falls at a known rate. It falls because plants no longer take in the isotope through **photosynthesis** and animals no longer take in the isotope by eating plants. All the time the isotope is decaying. The **half-life** of $^{14}_{6}C$ is 5730 years. By measuring the amount of radioactivity in a dead material it is possible to estimate the age of the material. The technique is used by archaeologists.

carbonate ($-CO_3$) The carbonate **group** has a **valency** of 2. Metal carbonates occur widely in nature, e.g. **limestone** ($CaCO_3$), **dolomite** ($CaMg(CO_3)_2$). and **malachite** ($CuCO_3.Cu(OH)_2$). Calcium carbonate plays a part in the **carbon cycle**.

Carbonates of all **metals** (except group I metals) are **insoluble** in **water**. All carbonates produce **carbon dioxide** when heated *strongly* (K_2CO_3, Na_2CO_3 with difficulty) and when treated with dilute **acid**. The chemical test of a carbonate is to add acid to the solid **compound** and to pass the **gas** produced through **lime-water**. A **precipitate**, seen as a milkiness, indicates that the **solid** was a carbonate.

carboxylic acid   An **organic acid** with the formula R—COOH. See **ethanoic acid**.

carcinogen   A **compound** which can cause cancerous growths in living cells.

β-carotene   Natural yellow colouring. It is found in carrots, egg yolk and butter and in all green leaves. It is now widely used as an **additive** in foods to provide yellow/orange colouring.

catalyser   Part of the exhaust system of modern **petrol** engines. A **platinum**/rhodium **catalyst** in a honeycomb structure converts carbon monoxide (CO), nitric oxide (NO) and unburnt **hydrocarbon** compounds from the **petrol** into **carbon dioxide** (CO_2), **nitrogen** (N_2) and nitrous oxide (N_2O). This is one way of reducing the amount of air **pollution** caused by the internal combustion engine.

Unleaded petrol must be used when a car is fitted with a catalyser otherwise the catalyst will be 'poisoned' by the **lead** and rendered useless.

See **greenhouse effect**, **greenhouse gases**, **ozone layer**.

catalysis See **catalyst**.

catalyst A substance which alters the **rate** of a chemical **reaction**. The catalyst remains unchanged at the end of the reaction. The process is called *catalysis*.

Transition metals and their **compounds** are often useful catalysts. Some examples are shown below:

Reaction	Catalyst
Haber process	**Iron**
Contact process	Vanadium(v) oxide (V_2O_5)
Ammonia→ nitric acid	**Platinum**-rhodium alloy
Hardening fats	Nickel

catalyst Transition metals used as catalysts.

The chemical processes which go on inside animals and plants are nearly all dependent on catalysts. These organic catalysts are called **enzymes**.

catalytic cracking See **cracking**.

cathode The negatively charged pole in a **battery** or **electrolysis cell**. Positively charged ions (**cations**) are attracted to the cathode during **electrolysis**. They gain electrons at the cathode.

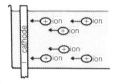

cathode Positive ions attracted to the negative cathode.

cation Positively charged **ions**. Most cations are **metal** ions, e.g. Fe^{2+}, Cr^{3+}, Na^+, Ca^{2+}, Al^{3+} and are attracted to the **cathode** during **electrolysis**. Three cations not formed from metals are the **hydrogen ion** (H^+) the **oxonium ion** (H_3O^+) and the **ammonium ion** (NH_4^+).

caustic Describes substances which burn or corrode **organic** material, e.g. flesh. It is usually restricted to use with **alkaline** materials, e.g. caustic soda (**sodium hydroxide**) and caustic potash (**potassium hydroxide**).

cell 1. A device for obtaining electrical **energy** from chemical **reactions**; often called a **battery**. 2. The single units from which large batteries are made, e.g. the lead-acid **accumulator** used in most cars contains six cells, each of which gives 2 volts. The total voltage is 12 volts as the cells are connected together in series in the accumulator. The common dry battery is a single cell.

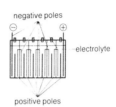

negative poles

electrolyte

positive poles

cell   A lead-acid accumulator.

3. Apparatus and chemicals which are used in **electrolysis**, e.g. *electrolytic cell*.

cellulose   A **carbohydrate** which is also a **polymer**. It is made up of **glucose monomers**. The **formula** is $(C_6H_{10}O_5)_n$ and is the material from which cell walls of plants are made. Cellulose is useful to us in several ways. It is used to manufacture **paper** and **rayon**.

Celsius scale of temperature (°C)   This scale of **temperature** is based on a 100° range between the **melting** point of pure **ice** (0°C) and the boiling point of **pure water** (100°C). Originally called the *centigrade* scale, it is now named after the

Swedish astronomer, Anders Celsius (1701–44), who devised it. One degree Celsius equals one **Kelvin**.

cement A substance made by heating **chalk** or **limestone** together and then powdering the product.

The result is a mixture of **calcium** silicate and calcium aluminate, which is usually a grey colour. When **water** is added a corrosive **mixture** is produced which is **alkaline**. Cement is a very important **adhesive** material in the building industry:

> cement + sand + water → **mortar**
>
> cement + sand + gravel + water → **concrete**

ceramic **Inorganic** material with the following properties:
(a) Great hardness and resistance to wear;
(b) Very high **melting** point;
(c) Chemically **inert**.
Ceramic materials include, **glass**, **enamel**, pottery, **clay** products, **abrasive** and **refractory** material.

CFC (chlorofluorocarbons) **Organic compound** which contains **carbon**, **chlorine** and **fluorine** atoms. CFC **molecules** were developed in the 1920s for use as refrigerants. They are stable, **inert**, odourless, non-toxic, non-corrosive and do not burn. After World War II, their use grew rapidly, for example, as propellants in **aerosol** containers, fire-extinguishing fluids, in (**synthetic**) **foam** production, and as fluids in air-conditioning systems and freezers.

In the mid-1970s, it became known that CFCs break down in the stratosphere and produce reactive **chlorine** atoms which then go on to react with **ozone** molecules. In this way, the amount of ozone in the stratosphere is reduced and we have less protection from the harmful effects of **ultraviolet radiation**. Now efforts are being made to reduce the use of CFCs, and to find substitutes for them which do not reduce the amount of ozone in the stratosphere. Unfortunately, some of the readily available alternatives are **greenhouse gases**. See **earth's atmosphere**.

chain Atoms of **carbon** that **bond** together in chains and form long **molecules**. In **polymers**, these chains can be thousands of atoms long. The chains can have branches too.

chain reaction A rapid series of **reactions** in which the product of each reaction causes the next one to occur. For example, some **isotopes** are unstable and when they are bombarded with a **neutron** they break up to produce smaller atoms and more neutrons (nuclear **fission**).

$$^{235}_{92}U + neutron \rightarrow \left\{ \begin{array}{l} \text{atoms of barium} \\ \text{and krypton} \end{array} \right\} + 3 \text{ neutrons}$$

Each time a neutron is used up, three more are produced, each of which can then go on to split up another large unstable atom and produce even more neutrons. These can then go on and more and more neutrons are produced. This is called a chain reaction and is the basis for **nuclear reactions** in nuclear power stations and atom bombs.

chalk   A rock which has been formed from the shells of marine animals. It is mainly **calcium carbonate** ($CaCO_3$). It is a softer rock than **limestone** and its uses are limited by this.

change of state   The movement of a material to and from the **solid**, **liquid** and **gas** states. Such movements are always accompanied by **energy** changes. See **kinetic theory** and **phase change**.

charcoal   A black substance made by heating **organic** material (usually wood) in the absence of **air**. In this process, **volatile** material escapes and the resulting charcoal is mainly composed of **carbon**. Before **coal** was widely available, charcoal was used to make **iron** from iron **ore**. Some charcoal, **active carbon** is able to adsorb small **molecules** onto its surface. This is used in gas masks, in the **sugar** refining industry and has other uses where coloured impurities need to be removed from materials.

Charles' law   The **volume** of a fixed **mass** of **gas** is dependent upon its **temperature**. If the temperature of a gas is doubled (measured on the **Kelvin** scale) then the volume of the gas will double — if the **pressure** of the gas is kept constant.

Named after the French physicist Jacques Charles, 1746–1823. See **Boyle's law**, **gas laws**.

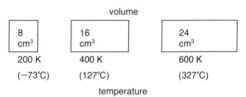

volume

8 cm³	16 cm³	24 cm³
200 K	400 K	600 K
(−73°C)	(127°C)	(327°C)

temperature

Charles' law Doubling the temperature of a gas doubles its volume.

chemical change A change in which one or more chemical substances are changed into *different* ones. Such a change is usually accompanied by the giving out or taking in of **heat energy**. See **physical change**.

chemical reaction See **reaction**.

china clay A complex **aluminium compound** formed by the decomposition of feldspar in **granite** rock. **China clay** is used in **paper** manufacture, and in the pottery and textile industries.

chipboard Material made from wood chippings which are held together by a glue or a resin. The **mixture** is rolled into sheets and allowed to dry. It is then cut to size. Faced with a **veneer**, chipboard is often used to make modern furniture. See **softboard**.

chlorides Compounds of **chlorine** and another **element**. **Metal** chlorides are usually **ionic** solids, e.g. sodium chloride (NaCl) and barium chloride ($BaCl_2$).

Non-metal chlorides are **covalent** compounds and are usually either low **boiling point** liquids such as tetrachloromethane (CCl_4) or gases such as hydrogen chloride (HCl).

Metal chlorides react with concentrated **acids** to produce **hydrogen chloride** gas:

$$H_2SO_4(l) + NaCl(s) \rightarrow NaHSO_4(s) + HCl(g)$$

The test for chlorides is to mix a **solution** with silver nitrate solution. If a white **precipitate** forms which then dissolves when **ammonia** solution is added the substance is a chloride.

chlorination The addition of **chlorine** to drinking **water** and to water used in swimming pools in order to kill dangerous bacteria. The term is also used to describe **reactions** between chlorine and **hydrocarbons** to produce chlorinated hydrocarbons.

chlorine   (Cl_2) A green **gas** at **room temperature**. It is a member of the **halogen** group of elements (**group** VII) and is very reactive. It has a choking effect and attacks lung tissue and the throat if it is breathed in. It was used as a chemical weapon in World War I.

Chlorine occurs naturally as **chlorides** and sodium chloride is abundant in seawater. Chlorine is extracted by the **electrolysis** of **rock salt** solutions. It is used widely to make **polymers**, **biocides**, **disinfectants** and **solvents**. A solution of chlorine in water is used as a **bleach**. See **chlorination**.

Chlorine is a vigorous **oxidizing agent** which readily reacts with most **elements**. It is made in the laboratory by the oxidation of concentrated hydrochloric acid:

$$4HCl(aq) + MnO_2(s) \rightarrow$$

$$Cl_2(g) + MnCl_2(aq) + 2H_2O(l)$$

chlorine

chloroethene (or **vinyl chloride**) The **monomer** from which **poly(chloroethene) (PVC) is made. It is made by reacting ethene** (C_2H_4) with **chlorine** (Cl_2).

C_2H_3Cl

(a)

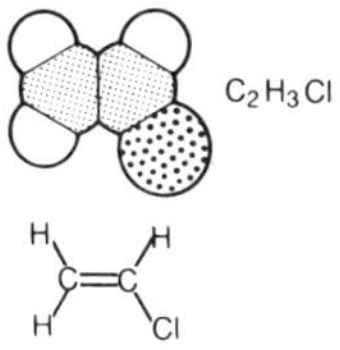

(b)

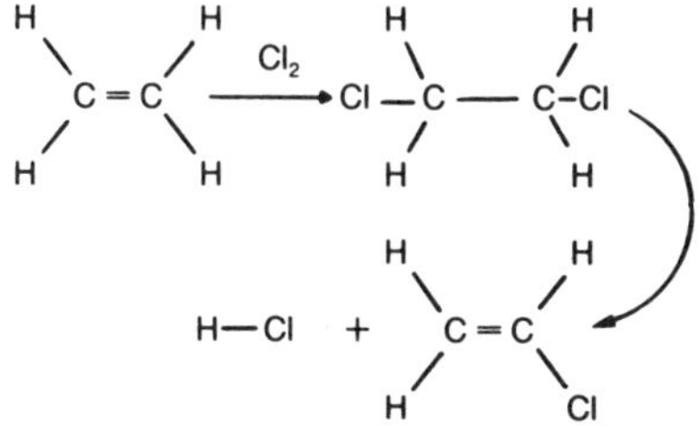

Chloroethene (a) the monomer, (b) reacting ethene with chlorine to make chloroethene.

chlorofluorocarbons   See **CFC**.

chlorophyll   The green pigment in plants which is responsible for the absorption of the Sun's **energy** by the plant. This **energy** is used in the process of **photosynthesis**. There are two kinds of chlorophyll, each of which is a complex **molecule** which contains a **magnesium** atom.

chromatography   A technique for separating **mixtures** of **solutes** in a **solution**. The process occurs because some materials cling to the paper more than others: in the example, dye B is more tightly held than A. The technique is widely used in **analysis**.

chromatography   A spot of dye is placed on filter paper (I); as the water moves out across the paper the dye separates (II) in different bands of colour.

chromium   A **transition metal**. It has important uses in **alloys**, e.g. **stainless steel**, and is used in chromium plating on items such as bicycle handlebars, kettles, car bumpers and cutlery. It is also used in the production of **pigments**, wood preservatives and in the tanning industry. It has a high resistance to corrosion. See **dichromate(VI) ion**, **electroplating**.

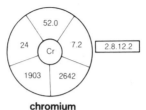

chromium

citric acid A weak organic **acid** (see **strengths of acids and bases**) which occurs naturally in *citrus* fruits such as oranges and lemons.

clay A natural material containing **aluminium**, **silicon** and **oxygen** atoms which is commonly found in soils. Clays are used in pottery making, in **ceramics** and as fillers in the manufacture of **rubber**, **paint**, **plastics** and **paper**. Clay has an important use as a lubricating mud during drilling for **minerals**. See **china clay**.

cm³ The abbreviation for cubic centimetre and a unit of **volume** used in scientific work. It is the volume of a cube which has a side of 1 cm. 1000 cm³ are equal to 1 litre or 1 cubic decimetre (1 **dm³**).

coal A fossilized plant material which was living millions of years ago. It has a very complex chemical structure containing **compounds** made up of **carbon, hydrogen, oxygen, nitrogen** and **sulphur**. **Coal** is used as a **fuel** in power stations, industry and the home and was, before the use of **natural gas**, used as the source of coal gas. About 20% of coal is used to make **coke**.

If coal is heated in the absence of **air**, coal tar is produced. In the middle of this century coal tar was an important source of **organic** chemicals, e.g. **phenol** from which dyes, drugs and **polymers** were made. Now over 90% of such products come from **petroleum** sources.

As the world has greater reserves of coal than **petroleum**, attempts are being made to convert coal into petroleum products.

cobalt A **transition metal**. It is a magnetic element and is used alloyed with **iron** in the manufacture of magnets. The radioactive **isotope** $^{60}_{27}$Co emits **gamma rays** and it is used in

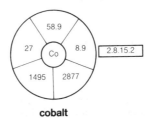

cobalt

the treatment of cancers. Cobalt(II) chloride is blue when **anhydrous** and pink when **hydrated**, and so the **compound** is used as a test for the presence of **water**.

coke The material left behind when the **volatile** compounds have been removed from **coal**. It contains over 80% **carbon**. It was made during the production of coal gas but now is made in *coke ovens* from special *coking coal*. Coke is used to make **carbon monoxide** in the **blast furnace** and is an important (smokeless) **fuel**.

combining power See **valency**.

combustion A burning **reaction** in which a substance combines with a **gas**. Heat and light (i.e. **flame**) usually accompany combustion **reactions**. Most combustions involve **oxygen**, e.g.:

$$2H_2(g) + O_2(g) \rightarrow 2H_2O(g)$$

complex ion A **cation** (e.g. **metal** ions or **hydrogen** ions) which is bonded to one or more small **molecules** by a **coordinate bond**. The simplest examples are the **ammonium ion** and the **oxonium ion**, where the **lone pair of electrons** on the **nitrogen** and **oxygen** atoms forms the bond.

Transition metal ions form a large number of complex ions because they can easily accept the donated **electron** pairs.

NH_4^+ H_3O^+

complex ions Ammonium and oxonium ions.

composite material A substance made up of layers of materials reinforced by **fibres** (e.g. **carbon**, **glass**). Composite materials are strong and have wide use in cars, planes, boats, furniture and sports gear.

compound A pure substance which is made up of two or more **elements** chemically bonded together. The **properties** of a compound are quite different from the properties of the **elements** bonded together within it. Compounds may contain **ionic** or **covalent** bonding. Examples are methane CH_4, water H_2O, sodium chloride NaCl. See **mixture**.

concentrated Containing a high proportion of something. A concentrated **solution** is one which contains a relatively large proportion of **solute**. If you want to increase the concentration of a solution, this can be done by either adding more solute or by removing **solvent** (e.g. by **distillation**) from the solution. See **dilute**.

concentration A measure of how much **solute** is **dissolved** in a **solution**. It is usually expressed in terms of how much substance is present in a given volume of the solution. This can either be in terms of **mass**, e.g. grammes, or in terms of how many particles, e.g. **moles**. Examples of concentrations and how they can be written are, for a solution containing 170 grammes of silver nitrate (1 mole) in one cubic decimetre (dm^3) of solution (see **molarity**):

170 g/dm^3, or 1 mol/dm^3 or 1 mol/l or 1 M.

concrete A building material made up of an **aggregate** (crushed stone, or **slag**) mixed with **cement**, **sand** and **water**.

condensation **1.** The change from the **gas** or **vapour** state to the **liquid** state, e.g. **water** condensing onto a cold window pane.
2. A **reaction** in which two or more **molecules** react to produce a larger molecule and a small molecule such as water. This is one method of producing **polymers**, such as **nylon**.

conductor A substance which allows heat or electricity to flow through it. An *electrical* conductor is a substance which will allow an electric **current** to flow through it. **Metals**, **solutions** which contain **ions**, and molten **ionic** compounds are conductors; all other substances are **insu-**

lators. **Graphite** (a form of **carbon**) is a notable exception. Certain **metalloids** are **semiconductors**.

The term 'conductor' is also applied to substances which allow **heat energy** to flow through them. Metals are also good conductors of heat.

conservation of energy and mass   Mass and energy cannot be created or destroyed in a chemical **reaction** because the mass of the reacting substances and the mass of the products are equal. They are *conserved*. Similarly:

| Energy possessed by reacting substances | = | Energy possessed by the products of the **reaction** | + | Any **heat energy** which is exchanged with the surroundings. |

These relationships are only approximations. The work of Einstein showed that mass and energy can be converted into each other. This is important in **nuclear reactions** but in ordinary chemical reactions the relationship holds good.

contact process   The method used to make almost all the **sulphuric acid** produced today. The flow chart shows the steps. Most sulphuric acid is now made from **sulphur**. The reactions marked * are **exothermic** and so the process is relatively cheap to run because little **heat energy** has to be supplied.

| sulphur | $S(s) + O_2(g) \rightarrow SO_2(g)^*$ |

or

| sulphide ores (e.g. ZnS) | reaction with **air** | | Sulphur dioxide SO_2 |
| | $2ZnS(s) + 3O_2(g) \rightarrow 2ZnO(s) + 2SO_2(g)$ | | |

reacted with **air** over a vanadium (V) oxide **catalyst** at 450°C to produce:
$2SO_2(g) + O_2(g) \rightarrow 2SO_3(g)^*$

| sulphuric acid H_2SO_4 (98%) | sulphur trioxide gas is absorbed* into concentrated sulphuric acid (98%) which is then diluted with water to keep the concentration at 98%: $H_2O(l) + SO_3(g) \rightarrow H_2SO_4(l)^*$ | | sulphur trioxide SO_3 |

contact process The steps in making sulphuric acid.

control A parallel experiment, carried out at the same time as a main experiment, in which the factor being investigated is kept constant. The result of the main experiment in which this factor is varied can be compared with the control to check the extent of any change.

coordinate bond A **covalent bond** in which *both* the **electrons** in the bonds have come from the *same* **atom**. Electrons have been *donated* by one atom rather than one donated from each atom. The bond is also known as a dative bond. In coordinate bonding, the donor atom uses a **lone pair of electrons**. See **complex ion**.

$$H-\overset{\displaystyle H}{\underset{\displaystyle H}{N}}: \;\rightarrow\; H^+ \;\rightarrow\; NH_4^+$$

coordinate bonds

copolymer A **polymer** made by the joint

polymerization of two (or more) kinds of **monomer**. Copolymers are **compounds** rather than **mixtures** and can be produced with particular **properties** in mind. They are widely used in industry to produce everyday objects. The fibre Acrilan is a good example.

copper   A **transient element** which plays an important part in our lives. It is a vital trace element in our bodies — we need between one and two milligrammes per day.

Copper is an unreactive metal, coming low down in the **electrochemical series**. It will not liberate **hydrogen** from dilute **acids**.

It can be purified by using the impure metal as the **anode** with copper(II) sulphate as the **electrolyte** and a small pure copper cathode in an **electrolysis cell**.

Copper metal is used in plumbing, for electrical wiring and for coinage. (Copper is an excellent **conductor**.) It is extracted commercially from its **sulphide** ores:

| Chalcopyrite | $(CuFeS_2)$ |
| Bornite | (Cu_5FeS_4) |

and its carbonate ores:

| Malachite | $(CuCO_3.Cu(OH)_2)$ |
| Azurite | $(2CuCO_3.Cu(OH)_2)$ |

Copper is also found as the free element, an indication of its lack of **reactivity**.

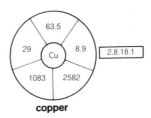

copper

copper compounds

Copper(II) chloride $CuCl_2.2H_2O$	Used to give fireworks a green colour and in the removal of **sulphur** from **petroleum**.
Copper(II) hydroxide $Cu(OH)_2$	Used in the manufacture of **rayon**, in dyeing textiles and as a blue pigment.
Copper(II) carbonate $CuCO_3$	Forms part of the ores malachite and azurite — both basic copper carbonates. Another basic carbonate — verdigris — is formed as a surface layer on copper which is exposed to the **atmosphere**.
Copper(II) sulphate $CuSO_4.5H_2O$	Forms blue **crystals** and can be made by treating copper compounds (oxide, carbonate, hydroxide) with dilute **sulphuric acid**. The **anhydrous** salt is a white powder which turns blue when water is added:

$$CuSO_4 + 5H_2O \rightarrow CuSO_4.5H_2O$$

white   blue

This reaction is often used as a test for the presence of **water**. The **compound** is used in wood preservatives and fungicides, e.g. Bordeaux mixture.

corrosion A process whereby stone or metal is chemically eaten away. Good examples are the weathering of **limestone** buildings by rainwaters, which contain dissolved **acids**, and the **rusting** of **steel**. Corrosion begins at the surface and often a surface layer protects the rest of the material, e.g. the **oxide** coating on **aluminium**. Rusting is not like this, the rusting process goes through the steel until it is all corroded. That is why it is so damaging and expensive. See **acid rain**.

cotton A natural **cellulose fibre** which forms strong and hard-wearing fabrics. Cotton is good to wear next to the skin in hot climates because of its ability to absorb **water**.

coulomb A measurement of **electric** charge. It is the product of the **current** (**units=ampère**) and the time (units=**seconds**), e.g. if a current of 0.6 amps flows for 10 seconds, 6 coulombs of electricity will have passed through the circuit.

Named after the French physicist Charles Augustin de Coulomb, 1736–1806, famous for his work with electricity and magnetism.

covalent bonds **Bonds** formed by two **atoms** coming together and sharing their **electrons**, e.g. **hydrogen** atoms have one electron each (●). The atoms form a **molecule** of hydrogen (H_2) by the two electrons forming a bond. Thus each 'shared pair' of electrons produces one covalent bond.

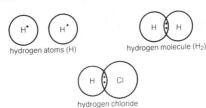

hydrogen atoms (H)

hydrogen molecule (H_2)

hydrogen chloride

covalent bonds Atoms of H_2 form a molecule by two electrons forming a bond.

Covalent bonds are usually found in **compounds** which only contain non-metallic elements, e.g.:

Carbon dioxide	CO_2
Hydrogen chloride	HCl
Nitrogen dioxide	NO_2
Ammonia	NH_3
Phosphorus(V) oxide	P_2O_5

and also in elements with an **atomicity** of two or more, e.g.:

Oxygen	O_2	Hydrogen	H_2
Bromine	Br_2	Chlorine	Cl
Nitrogen	N_2	Sulphur	S_8
Ozone	O_3	Phosphorus	P_4

Covalent bonds which contain two electrons, i.e. one 'shared pair' are termed *single* bonds. Many molecules contain **double** or **triple** bonds. Covalent bonds are not as strong as **ionic bonds**.

covalent compounds Compounds which contain **covalent bonds**. They tend to be non-**conductors**. Their **melting** and **boiling points** are low when present in **molecules**. **Giant structures** which contain covalent bonds, however, have high melting and boiling points.

cracking The process in which large **hydrocarbon molecules** are broken up into small molecules. This occurs in the **petroleum**-refining industry. Small molecules are more valuable than large ones because they are the starting materials needed in the production of other chemicals such as **polymers**, e.g. **poly(ethene)** and **poly(propene)**, and **fuels**, such as **petrol** and **diesel fuel**.

Different products are formed from different raw materials under different conditions, as shown in the table overleaf.

cross-linking Chemical **bonds** formed between **polymer** molecules lying side by side.

Conditions	Process name	Products
High temperature	Thermal cracking	**Unsaturated** and **saturated** molecules are produced
High temperature in the presence of **steam**	Steam cracking	
High temperature in the presence of a catalyst	Catalytic cracking	
High temperature and pressure in the presence of **hydrogen**	Hydro-cracking	The product is totally saturated

cracking Different processes and their products.

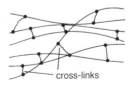
cross-links

cross-linking Chemical bonds formed between polymer molecules.

Cross-linking within **molecules** produces materials which:
(a) Have higher **relative molecular masses**;
(b) Are tougher and less flexible;
(c) Have higher **melting** points;
(d) Are less soluble.
Examples of materials which are extensively cross-linked include rubber which has undergone **vulcanization**, **Bakelite** and similar polymers and **epoxy resins**.

crude oil   See **petroleum**.

cryolite   A **mineral**. In the extraction of **aluminium**, **bauxite** (Al_2O_3) is dissolved in molten cryolite ($3 NaF.AlF_3$) at 900°C and the **mixture** is then electrolysed. Aluminium is produced at the **cathode**. Cryolite only occurs naturally in Greenland. The amounts needed in the extraction of aluminium have to be produced by the reaction between aluminium oxide (Al_2O_3) and hydrogen fluoride (HF).

crystal   A **solid** substance that has its **atoms** (**molecules** or **ions**) arranged in a set geometrical three-dimensional pattern (see overleaf). The shape of these atomic arrangements (crystal **lattices**) determines the shapes that the solid has when it undergoes **crystallization**.

cubic   octahedral   tetrahedral

crystal Examples of different crystal arrangements.

crystallization The process in which **crystals** are formed. In nature, crystals are produced when molten rocks cool down and solidify. In laboratory experiments, crystals are usually produced from a **solution**. There are two main methods:

(a) A solution is left at **room temperature**. Slow **evaporation** of the **solvent** takes place and crystals are left behind.

(b) A **supersaturated solution** is made *above* room temperature. As this is cooled down, crystals are produced.

curing 1. A word used to describe the hardening of resins.
2. A method of preserving meats such as bacon, ham, gammon and beef. The curing **solution** usually consists of a **mixture** of **sodium salts** and is either rubbed onto or injected into the raw meat.

current The movement of **electrons** through a **conductor**. It is measured in **ampères** (amps).

Electric current is said to move from the positive terminal to the negative terminal. The electrons, however, travel from the negative terminal to the positive. This difference is because the electron carries a negative electric charge.

cyanides   A range of compounds which contain the −CN group of atoms. Potassium cyanide (K^+CN^-) and hydrogen cyanide ($H−C≡N$) are the best known examples. They are very poisonous. Cyanides prevent the flow of **energy** within the body and so are effective very quickly.

DC (or **direct current**)   The type of electrical **current** produced from a simple **cell** or **battery**. Only DC can be used in **electrolysis**.

DDT (or   **DichloroDiphenylTrichloroethane**)   A widely used **pesticide** which has been successful in the control of diseases such as malaria. It is, however, harmful to animal life as some animals can concentrate it in their bodies where it acts as a **poison**. For this reason many countries now restrict its use.

DDT

decomposition The break up of **compounds** into simpler compounds or into **elements**. Usually **heat** is needed (thermal decomposition), e.g.

$$2Cu(NO_3)_2(s) \rightarrow 2CuO(s) + 4NO_2(g) + O_2(g)$$

$$2HgO(s) \rightarrow 2Hg(l) + O_2(g)$$

$$CaCO_3(s) \rightarrow CaO(s) + CO_2(g)$$

dehydrating agent A substance which is used to remove **water** from other substances. Such substances always have an attraction for water. They can be substances which dissolve in water, e.g.:

| Concentrated sulphuric acid H_2SO_4 | Sodium hydroxide NaOH |

or substances which react with water, e.g.:

| Calcium oxide CaO | this forms the hydroxide $\rightarrow Ca(OH)_2$ |

A third kind of dehydrating agent is the **anhydrous** salt which absorbs water, e.g.:

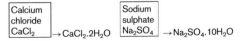

| Calcium chloride $CaCl_2$ | $\rightarrow CaCl_2.2H_2O$ | Sodium sulphate Na_2SO_4 | $\rightarrow Na_2SO_4.10H_2O$ |

Dehydrating agents are used in **desiccators**.

dehydration A chemical **reaction** which takes place by the removal of a **molecule** of **water**. The water molecule can be chemically combined as **water of crystallization**, or can come from chemical change within the molecule. Examples include:

$$CaSO_4.2H_2O(s) \rightarrow CaSO_4(s)$$

$$\text{concentrated } H_2SO_4$$
$$C_6H_{12}O_6(s) \rightarrow 6C(s) + 6H_2O(g)$$

deliquescence Substances that are able to take in **water** from the **atmosphere**. They can take in so much water that they are able to form a **solution** — unlike **hygroscopic** substances. Some common examples are:

Iron(III) chloride $FeCl_3$	Copper(II) nitrate $Cu(NO_3)_2$	Calcium chloride $CaCl_2$

Some deliquescent substances are used in **desiccators**.

delocalized electrons In normal **covalent bonds**, **electrons** are found between two **atoms**, e.g. a carbon-carbon **single bond** consists of two electrons: $C:C$, and a double bond contains four electrons: $C::C$. These electrons are located in between the atoms. They are *localized*. In some substances, however, there are some electrons which are free to move amongst the atoms. These electrons are *delocalized*. **Graphite** contains delocalized electrons within the hexagonal layers of atoms. This is why graphite can conduct electricity along the layers but not between them. **Metals** have delocalized electrons too and this explains their being good **conductors**.

density The density of a substance is a measure of how much space a certain amount of the substance takes up. The smaller the space into which the **mass** is **concentrated**, the *greater* is the density. The density of a substance, e.g. **lead**, is determined by the density of the individual **atoms** *and* by how closely together the atoms are arranged in the **crystal lattice**. Generally speaking, the more particles that an atom contains, the denser it will be.

Density is calculated by dividing a substance's mass by its **volume**. The units are usually either g/**cm**^{3} or kg/m^3.

desiccator A device used to store substances which need a dry **atmosphere**, e.g. **deliquescent** or **hygroscopic** substances.

A desiccator is airtight and contains a **dehydrating agent** which makes the air dry.

desulphurization The removal of **compounds** of **sulphur** from **petroleum**, **natural gas** or other **fossil fuels** before use. Desulphurization not only prevents the release of the acidic pollutant **sulphur dioxide**, but also allows the sulphur which is recovered to be sold. The sulphur is usually removed by using **hydrogen** and a **catalyst** to form a **hydrocarbon** and hydrogen sulphide (H_2S). The H_2S is then treated chemically to produce sulphur. 95% recovery is possible with these methods.

detergent A cleaning agent also known as a *surfactant*. It does two things when used in washing, e.g. clothes or dishes. It reduces the surface tension of the water and so allows the water to wet things more thoroughly. It also acts to bring together the water and (normally insoluble) **fat**, **oil** or grease into an **emulsion**. If the presence of a detergent is accompanied by rapid movement, e.g. in a washing machine, then particles of dirt and grit are removed and the article is cleaned.

Detergents form an emulsion because one part of their molecule is **ionic** and is attracted to water and because the other part (the **hydrocarbon** chain) is attracted to the oil molecules. Detergents, thus, hold the two together.

detergent A synthetic detergent molecule.

See **soap**, **hydrophilic** and **hydrophobic**.

- 12%   detergent
- 40%   builders such as polyphosphates to remove calcium and magnesium ions from the water
- 12%   bleach such as sodium perborate
- 20%   anti-caking chemical to make sure that the powder runs smoothly
- 10%   water
- 5%   other substances such as dyes, enzymes, perfume
- 1%   suspension agent to keep the dirt suspended in the water

detergent Contents of a typical packet of powder for an automatic washing-machine.

deuterium An **isotope** of **hydrogen** which has a **neutron** and a **proton** in the **nucleus**. Its symbol is written:

$$^2_1H \text{ or } ^2_1D.$$

The isotope occurs naturally, making up 0.015% of hydrogen. Because its density is twice that of normal hydrogen it is easily separated.

Deuterium oxide is known as *heavy water* and its formula is written D_2O.

di- A prefix which means *two*. For example:
(a) Carbon *di*oxide CO_2 — two **atoms** of **oxygen**.
(b) *di*atomic molecule — two atoms in the molecule.

diamond A valuable **mineral** which is an **allotrope** of **carbon**. It occurs naturally, mainly in South Africa and the Soviet Union. It is the hardest naturally occurring substance known and is used in drill tips and saw blades. Diamond is prized as a gemstone because of its rarity and the sparkle it produces. The carbon **atoms** are arranged in the **crystal lattice** in a **tetrahedral** formation and are **covalently bonded** to each other.

diatomic molecule A **molecule** which contains *two* (**di-**) atoms, e.g.

$$N_2 \quad O_2 \quad H_2 \quad Cl_2 \quad F_2 \quad Br_2 \quad I_2.$$

diaphragm cell An electrochemical **cell** for the production of **chlorine** and **sodium hydroxide** from **brine**. In the cell, the **anode** and **cathode** are separated by a porous membrane, called a *diaphragm*, which prevents the **chlorine** formed at the anode from reacting with the sodium hydroxide formed at the cathode. This means of producing chlorine and sodium hydroxide is now coming back into greater use because it does not involve the use of **mercury**.

dibasic acid An **acid** which contains *two* (**di-**) replaceable **hydrogen** atoms per molecule.

An example is shown below. With such acids, two kinds of salt can be formed — the *normal* salt, in which *both* hydrogen atoms are replaced, and the **acid salt** in which only one hydrogen has been replaced.

Acid	Salts	
	acid	*normal*
H_2SO_4 sulphuric acid	$NaHSO_4$ sodium hydrogen-sulphate	Na_2SO_4 sodium sulphate

dichromate(VI) ion ($Cr_2O_7{}^{2-}$) An **ion** which contains **chromium** and **oxygen** atoms and has a **valency** of 6. Its formula is $Cr_2O_7{}^{2-}$ and it is usually used as the bright orange **potassium** or **ammonium** salts:

$$K_2Cr_2O_7 \quad (NH_4)_2Cr_2O_7$$

Dichromate ion is an **oxidizing agent** which is reduced to **chromium**(III) ions Cr^{3+}.

diesel fuel　A **fuel/air mixture** is injected into diesel engines where it is compressed. The **temperature** produced in the compression causes the fuel/air mixture to explode. The fuel is produced from **petroleum** and is made up mainly of **alkanes** in the boiling range 200–350°C. It is often sold as 'DERV' fuel: *D*iesel, *E*ngine, *R*oad, *V*ehicle.

diethyl ether　See **ethers**.

diffusion　The complete mixing of two **gases** (e.g. **air** and **nitrogen dioxide**) that are at first separated and then allowed to mix. This happens because the molecules in the gases are moving about randomly at high speed because of the **thermal energy** they possess.

Diffusion occurs at a faster rate when the temperature is raised. The *less* dense a gas is, the *greater* is its rate of diffusion (see **density**). Diffusion also occurs in **liquids**, **solutions** and **solids**.

dilute solution　A **solution** which contains a relatively low **concentration** of solute. If you want to make a solution *more* dilute it is usual to add more solvent to it. Dilute **acids** usually have concentrations of 2 **mol/dm**^{3} or *less*.

dimer　A **molecule** which is made up of two

identical molecules (**monomers**) which are bonded together.

dimer An example of N_2O_4 as a dimer of NO_2.

disaccharide A **sugar** molecule which is made up of two **monosaccharide** sugar **molecules** which have undergone a **condensation** reaction with the elimination of a molecule of water.

Monosaccharides	Disaccharide
glucose + glucose $C_6H_{12}O_6$ $C_6H_{12}O_6$	maltose $C_{12}H_{22}O_{11}$
glucose + fructose $C_6H_{12}O_6$ $C_6H_{12}O_6$	sucrose $C_{12}H_{22}O_{11}$

disaccharide Monosaccharide sugars which form disaccharides after condensation.

disinfectant A substance capable of destroying harmful bacteria. They are often based on the **compound phenol**.

displacement reaction A reaction in which a less reactive element is displaced by a more

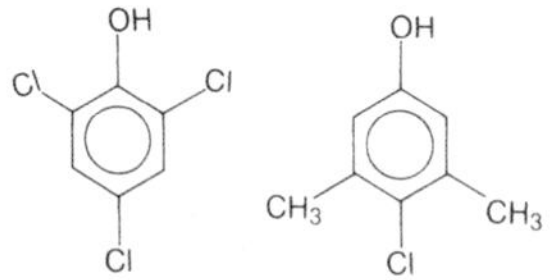

used in
T.C.P.

used in
Dettol

disinfectant Two common household disinfectants.

reactive one. These are **redox** reactions. For example:

$$CuSO_4(aq) + Zn(s) \rightarrow ZnSO_4(aq) + Cu(s)$$

$$2NaBr(aq) + Cl_2(g) \rightarrow 2NaCl(aq) + Br_2(aq)$$

dissociation The breaking up of a **compound** into smaller simpler **molecules** or **ions**. The dissociation is sometimes **reversible**.

$$NH_4Cl(s) \underset{cool}{\overset{heat}{\leftrightarrows}} NH_3(g) + HCl(g)$$

ammonium   ammonia   hydrogen
chloride   chloride

dissolve To become mixed with and absorbed in a liquid. When a **solute** dissolves in a **solvent** to form a **solution** it is dispersed throughout the whole **volume** of the solvent. The **structure** of the solute is broken up.

distillation The process by which a **solvent** can be recovered from a **solution** or a **mixture**. The solution is heated and the solvent is turned into a **vapour**. The vapour is led away from the hot **flask** into a condenser where it cools and condenses to a liquid, and is collected. In this way pure solvent can be recovered. See **Fractional distillation**, **condensation**.

distilled water Tap **water** and rain water are not **pure**. They contain dissolved **salts** and **gases**. Water is often distilled to increase its purity. Most of the **salts** are left behind but the water still may contain dissolved **gases**. The presence of **carbon dioxide** reduces the **pH** of the water considerably.

dm^3 The symbol for cubic decimetre, 1000 **cm^3** $= 1$ dm^3.

dolomite A common **mineral** containing **calcium** carbonate ($CaCO_3$) and **magnesium** carbonate ($MgCO_3$). It is an important source of **magnesium** and is used in furnace linings.

double bond A chemical **bond** which contains *two shared pairs* of **electrons**. Carbon-carbon double bonds are found in **alkene** molecules. The presence of the extra electrons makes the **alkenes** very reactive. Such **compounds** which contain double (and **triple**) bonds are said to be **unsaturated** compounds. Examples are:

Oxygen $O = O$

Ethene

$$\overset{\displaystyle H}{\underset{\displaystyle H}{}} C = C \overset{\displaystyle H}{\underset{\displaystyle H}{}}$$

Carbon dioxide $O = C = O$

double decomposition (or **precipitation reactions**) This process occurs when ionic substances react in **solution**. The product is an insoluble **solid**. For example:

$$CaCl_2(aq) + Na_2CO_3(aq) \rightarrow CaCO_3(s) + 2NaCl(aq)$$

$$or\ Ca^{2+}(aq) + CO_3{}^{2-}(aq) \rightarrow CaCO_3(s)$$

This is a method of preparing insoluble **salts**.

dry cell A **battery** in which the **electrolyte** is in the form of a paste and so cannot spill from the battery. The only common *wet* battery used today is the lead-acid **accumulator**.

dry cleaning A process for cleaning fabrics which cannot safely be washed using **water**. The cleaning agents used are **hydrocarbon** compounds containing **chlorine**.

dry ice Solid **carbon dioxide**. This material **sublimes** and hence the name *dry*. It is used for keeping things cold (sublimation point$=-40°C$) and in the theatre for producing smoke and cloud effects on stage.

drying agent A substance used to extract the **water** from another material. Drying agents can also be used to keep substances dry and will often be packaged inside devices such as cameras. Examples are calcium oxide (CaO) and **silica gel**. See **dehydrating agent**.

ductile Easily shaped. A ductile substance can easily be drawn into wires, e.g. **copper** is a very ductile **metal**. The term is usually used only about metals. Ductile metals have large **crystals** within them. See **annealing**, **malleable**.

duralumin An **alloy** of **aluminium**. It contains **copper** (4%) and traces of **manganese**, **magnesium** and **silicon**. The alloy is much harder and stronger than the **pure metal**. It is used for the production of aircraft frames and cooking utensils.

dyes Chemicals which can be mixed or reacted with materials to make a coloured product, e.g. fabrics, **plastics**. The colour is produced because the dye absorbs some of the light which falls upon it and radiates the rest. See **pigment**.

dynamite An explosive invented by Alfred Nobel, 1833–96. He discovered that if the unstable explosive nitroglycerine was absorbed into a clay called *kieselguhr* the result was a *stick* of explosive which was safe until it was detonated. See **explosion**.

Earth's structure The Earth is made up of a crust, the mantle and a core. The crust is a relatively thin layer which varies in thickness from about 7 km under the sea to about 40 km under the continents; the top metre or so is soil. The mantle is about 2870 km thick and is made up of a molten layer held between two more rigid layers. The core is about 3500 km thick and is made up mainly of iron and nickel.

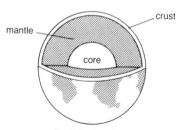

Earth's structure

Earth's atmosphere The mixture of **gases** surrounding the earth which protects us from harmful radiation from the **sun** and deep space, and provide part of the means of sustaining life on the planet. On earth, this **mixture** of gases is called **air**.

The **atmosphere** is over 1000 km deep, although over 90% of the air is found in the first 17 km. It is made up of several layers: the thermosphere, mesophere, stratosphere and troposphere. See **greenhouse effect**, **global warming**.

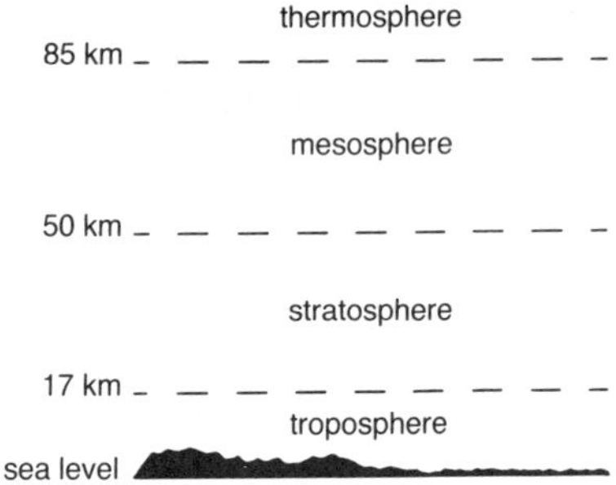

thermosphere

85 km _ — — — — — — — — —

mesosphere

50 km _ — — — — — — — — —

stratosphere

17 km _ — — — — — — — — —

troposphere

sea level

Earth's atmosphere   The layers making up the atmosphere.

efflorescence   The process in which **crystals** lose part of their **water of crystallization** when they stand in the **air**. They go powdery on their surfaces. A well known example of this process is sodium carbonate (washing soda):

$$Na_2CO_3.10H_2O(s) \rightarrow Na_2CO_3(s) + 10H_2O(g)$$

elastomer Material (usually a **polymer**) with *elastic* **properties**; in other words, the ability to stretch and return to its original shape. Examples are **synthetic** and natural **rubber**.

electric arc process See **steel manufacture**.

electric current or **electricity** See **current**.

electrochemical series **Elements** differ in their reactivity. When a **metal** is dipped into a **solution** of one of its salts, e.g. **zinc** in zinc sulphate solution, the following **reaction** occurs:

zinc $\rightarrow$ zinc ions + 2 electrons

$$Zn(s) \rightarrow Zn^{2+}(aq) + 2e^-$$

The **ions** go into solution and the **electrons** cling to the metal. If the metal and solution are made part of a circuit the electrons will flow round the circuit. The more reactive a metal is the greater the *force* with which the electrons move.

The series is useful because it allows us to compare reactivities and hence predict **reactions**, e.g.:
(a) Zinc *will* remove the oxygen from copper(II) oxide, but

(b) Copper *will not* remove oxygen from zinc oxide;

(c) Hydrogen *will* reduce copper(II) oxide *but not* zinc oxide

(d) Copper *will not* react with acids to release hydrogen.

K	potassium	↑
Na	sodium	
Ca	calcium	
Mg	magnesium	
Al	aluminium	
Zn	zinc	reactivity *increases*
Fe	iron	
Pd	lead	
H	hydrogen	
Cu	copper	
Ag	silver	

electrode A **conductor** which dips into an **electrolyte** and allows the **current** (**electrons**) to flow to and from the electrodes. **Copper, carbon** and **platinum** are used in **electrolysis** as electrodes. In electrolysis chemical reactions occur *at* the electrodes. See **anode**, **cathode**.

electrolysis A process in which a direct electric **current** (**DC**) is passed through a **liquid** which contains **ions** (an **electrolyte**) to produce **chemical changes** at the **electrodes**. Electrolysis is used to extract metals and non-metals from **compounds**. **Aluminium**, **sodium**, **chlorine** and

copper are produced in this way. For example:

At the anode	At the cathode
$Cl^- \rightarrow Cl + e^-$	$H^+ + e^- \rightarrow H$
$2Cl \rightarrow Cl_2$	$2H \rightarrow H_2$
chlorine is given off	hydrogen is given off

electrolyte   Either a molten ionic compound:

$$NaCl(l)   Pbl_2(l)$$

or a **solution** which contains **ions**:

$$HCl(aq)   NaOH(aq)   Kl(aq)   CuSO_4(aq)$$

Chemical changes take place when a direct electric **current** is passed through an electrolyte (**electrolysis**).

With molten **compounds** such as sodium chloride the changes are simple:

$$2Na^+Cl^-(l) \rightarrow 2Na(l) + Cl_2(g)$$

The elements are produced.

With ionic solutions, the processes are more complex. The products depend on the **concentration** of the solution, the voltage which is applied, the type of **electrode** which is used, and the nature of the ions present in the solution.

Electrolyte	Anode	Reaction
$CuSO_4(aq)$	(a) carbon or platinum	$4OH^-(aq) \rightarrow$ $2H_2O(l) + O_2(g) + 4e^-$
	(b) copper	$Cu(s) \rightarrow Cu^{2+}(aq) + 2e^-$

electrolyte Examples of electrolytes produced according to concentration of the solution. (a) **oxygen** is released, (b) the copper anode dissolves. Process (b) is used in the purification of **copper**.

electron A very small particle with an extremely tiny **mass** (about $\frac{1}{1840}$ of that of the **proton**). Electrons have a negative charge and move round the nuclei of **atoms**. They are given the symbol e^-.

When atoms lose or gain electrons they form **ions**:

gain→ negative **anions**, e.g. Cl^- O^{2-} Br^- S^{2-}

lose→ positive **cations**, e.g. Na^+ H^+ Fe^{2+} Al^{3+}

An electric **current** is electrons moving through a **conductor**. The way in which electrons are located in an atom is known as the **electronic configuration**.

electronegativity The power that an atom has to attract **electrons** to itself in a chemical **bond**.

Li	Be	B	C	N	O	F
Na						Cl
K						Br
Rb						I
Cs						At

electronegativity Example from the **periodic table** to show how electronegativity increases *across* a period and *up* a group.

It follows that **fluorine** has the most electronegative atoms.

electronic configuration A configuration is an *arrangement*. **Electrons** move around the **nucleus** of an **atom**. The movement takes place in clearly-defined regions (*orbitals*) in the atoms. Electrons are pictured as being arranged in orbits, or what are called **shells**, each of which can contain a *maximum* number of electrons.

Shell number:	①	②	③	④	⑤
Maximum number of electrons:	2	8	18	32	50

As we go across the **periodic table** the number of electrons increases by one per atom as the **atomic number** increases. The shells are filled up in turn — ① first, then ②, etc. — so that the electrons go into the region of the atom which has the lowest **energy.** For some elements described in this book, the electronic configuration is

given, e.g. sodium: 2·8·1. In other words, the ①
and ② shells are full and the ③ shell is beginning to fill.

Different configuration patterns are found in
the periodic table, e.g. **group** I elements always
have an electronic configuration ending in 1:

| Lithium | 2·1 |
| Sodium | 2·8·1 |

The **halogens** group VII have a different pattern;
this ends in 7 (the group number).

Fluorine	2·7
Chlorine	2·8·7
Bromine	2·8·18·7

electroplating A method of coating one metal
with a thin layer of another metal. The metallic
object to be coated is made the **cathode** and
undergoes **electrolysis** in a bath where the
electrolyte contains ions of the coating metal.
The **current**, electrolyte concentration and
temperature must be carefully controlled, as
they affect the deposited metal.

Electroplating is usually carried out either for
protection, e.g. chromium plating on handlebars
and motor cars and tin plating on cans, or for
decoration, e.g. silver plating cutlery and ornaments, and gold plating jewellery, etc.

electrostatic precipitation A method of removing dust from flue **gases** and other waste products. Gases are passed through a chamber which has a positive electrical charge (about 10 kilovolts). The negatively charged dust particles are attracted to the sides of the chamber and in this way the gas is cleaned.

electrovalent bond See **ionic bond**.

element A **pure** substance which cannot be broken down into anything simpler by chemical means. There are 104 elements known to us. Most of these occur naturally on the earth but several have been made in laboratories by **nuclear reactions**. All elements have a unique number of **protons** in their atoms. There are three classes of element:
(a) **Metals**, e.g. **iron**;
(b) **Non-metals**, e.g. **oxygen**;
(c) **Metalloids**, e.g. **arsenic**.

elementary particle The subatomic particles found in the **atom**. They are the **proton**, **neutron** and **electron**.

emery Aluminium oxide (Al_2O_3). It is used as an **abrasive**.

empirical formula The formula of a compound

which shows the atoms that are present in the molecule in their simplest ratio.

Compound	Molecular formula	Empirical formula
Ethene	C_2H_4	CH_2
Butane	C_4H_{10}	C_2H_5
Propane*	C_3H_8	C_3H_8
Ethanoic acid	$C_2H_4O_2$	CH_2O

> **empirical formula** Comparisons of the empirical and molecular formula of compounds (*note that the formulae for propane are the same).

See **molecular formula**, **percentage composition**.

emulsifier A substance which prevents an **emulsion** separating into layers. There are many natural emulsifiers; these and artificial **additives** are widely used in foods, cosmetics and medicines.

emulsion A mixture of **oil** and **water** which does not separate into layers. Milk is an emulsion with fat particles spread throughout the **liquid**. Salad cream and mayonnaise are emulsions of oil in **vinegar**. A natural **emulsifier** in egg yolk helps to keep the emulsion stable.

enamel A thin **glass** coating which is applied to materials such as **metals** to provide a protective and decorative coating. See **ceramic**.

endothermic reaction A reaction in which **heat energy** is taken in from the surroundings when a reaction occurs. There is either a fall in temperature when the reaction occurs, e.g. when sodium nitrate dissolves in water:

$$NaNO_3(s) \rightarrow NaNO_3(aq)$$

or heat energy has to be continually supplied to make a reaction occur, e.g.:

$$CaCO_3(s) \rightarrow CaO(s) + CO_2(g)$$

In endothermic reactions, there is *more* **energy** in the bonds of the products than there was in the **bonds** of the reactants.

end point The point at which a reaction is complete. The end point of a **titration** is when *all* of one of the reactants has been used up. The end point can be identified by an **indicator** or an instrument such as a **pH** meter or a conductivity meter.

energy The 'ability to do useful work'. Energy is *locked* inside the nuclei of **atoms**. Sometimes this can be released (see **nuclear reactions**). Energy is also found in the **bonds** between atoms. When chemicals react bonds break and new ones form. In this breaking and forming, energy can be *absorbed* or *released* as heat energy (see **energy change**). But in batteries it is released as electrical energy. Energy is usually measured in **joules** or **kilojoules**. See **enthalpy**.

energy change When chemical reactions occur, **heat energy** can be released from the reactants — they are **exothermic**; or can be taken in by the reactants — they are **endothermic**.

Energy changes are measured in **joules** or **kilojoules** and refer to a particular amount of substance, usually a **mole**. So, the energy change for the **Haber process** is −92 kilojoules per **mole** (−92 kJ/mol).

enthalpy The amount of **heat energy** possessed by a chemical substance. It is given the symbol H. It cannot be measured but, when chemicals react, the difference in the heat energy between the reactants and products can be measured by using a **thermometer**. This difference is the enthalpy change and is given the symbol ΔH. ΔH is negative for an **exothermic** reaction and positive for an **endothermic** one.

enzymes Usually **protein** molecules. They are **catalysts** which are found in living tissue. They allow complicated biochemical **reactions** to

equation 105

occur at low **temperatures** and **pressures** inside the body. It is thought that an enzyme is a particular shape which allows two reacting **molecules** to come close together on the enzyme. This makes the reaction easy to carry out.

epoxy resins Strong, **inert polymers** which are electrical **insulators**. They have wide uses as **adhesives**, coatings and **composite** materials. The resins are produced when and where needed by mixing a **poly(ether)** with a chemical reagent.

equation In chemistry, a way of describing a reaction. The equation can be a *word* equation:

$$\text{hydrogen} + \text{oxygen} \rightarrow \text{water}$$

or it can be a **formula** (or **symbol**) equation:

$$H_2 + O_2 \rightarrow H_2O$$

An equation is said to be *balanced* if there are the same number of each kind of **atom** on each side of the equation. For example:

$$2H_2 + O_2 \rightarrow 2H_2O$$

is a balanced equation.

Two **molecules** of **hydrogen** react with one molecule of **oxygen** to produce two molecules of **water**. It also tells us that 2 moles or 4 g of hydrogen react with 1 mole or 32 g of oxygen to produce 2 moles or 36 g of water. Since relative atomic mass $H = 1$, $O = 16$:

$$2H_2 + O_2 \rightarrow 2H_2O$$

$$2(2) + 32 = 2(2 + 16) = 36$$

Sometimes we use **ionic equations**:

$$Cu^{2+} + Zn \rightarrow Cu + Zn^{2+}$$

State symbols are usually added after the formula to denote which **state of matter** the substance is in. For example, gaseous hydrogen and oxygen react to produce liquid water:

$$2H_2(g) + O_2(g) \rightarrow 2H_2O(l)$$

equilibrium A state of balance or rest. In a **reversible reaction** the **reaction** proceeds in both directions:

$$3Fe(s) + 4H_2O(g) \rightleftharpoons Fe_3O_4(s) + 4H_2(g)$$

The reactants (**iron and steam**) produce the **oxide** and **hydrogen**. As soon as the products are made, they begin to react to reform steam and iron. There eventually comes a time when the **rate** of the forward$\rightarrow$reaction equals the rate of the reverse$\leftarrow$reaction. At this point the proportion of substances present is constant. There seems to be no reaction taking place. There is an equilibrium between the forward and reverse reactions.

It is important to realize that such an equilibrium is *dynamic*, that is, it produces motion. However, in an equilibrium, the reactions are occurring but, because they are taking place at the same rate, no change can be seen. Many important reactions involve equilibria.

In the **Haber process**, with the usual operating conditions, less than 20% of the **hydrogen** and **nitrogen** are converted into **ammonia**. This is the equilibrium **yield** of ammonia in the reaction.

essential fatty acid A **fatty acid** which is needed in the human diet because the body does not produce any or enough of it. There are four main essential fatty acids, all of which are found in vegetable oils.

ester A **compound** formed between an **alcohol** and a carboxylic **acid**. A **strong acid catalyst** is usually needed for the reaction.

Esters often have sweet, fruit smells and are used in perfumes, flavourings and essences.

The reaction between acid and alcohol is known as *esterification*.

ethane An **alkane**. It is colourless, flammable gas which is found in all **natural gas** (35% of North Sea gas). **Ethene** is formed when ethane is subjected to **cracking**.

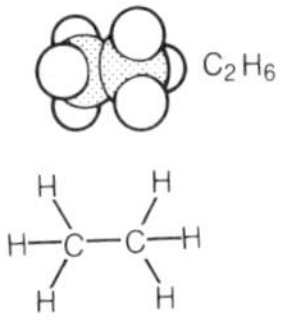

C_2H_6

ethane

ethanoic acid (or **acetic acid**) A colourless liquid (**melting point** 16°C, **boiling point** 118°C).

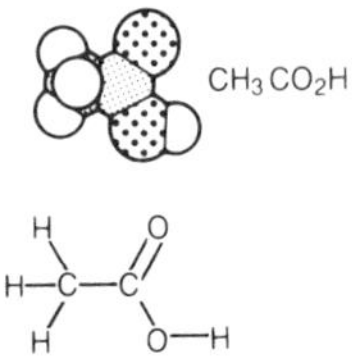

CH_3CO_2H

It is a **carboxylic acid** which is made industrially by the oxidation of **naphtha**. It is used to produce **esters** and other chemicals which are used to make **polymers** from which fabrics are made.

Ethanoic acid is present in **vinegar** (about a 4% aqueous solution). Although it is a **weak acid**, in a concentrated form it can cause severe skin burns.

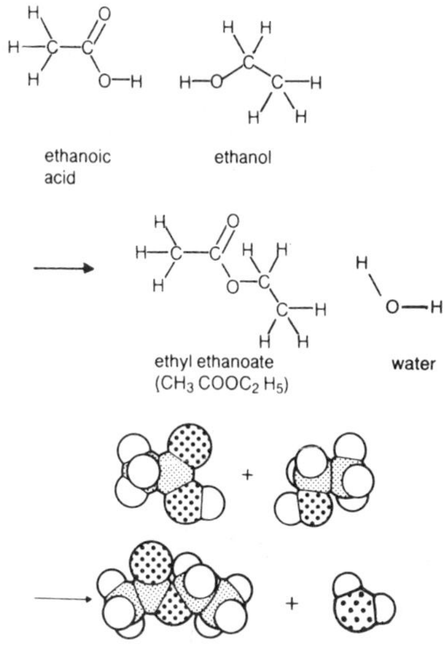

ethanoic
acid

ethanol

ethyl ethanoate
($CH_3 COOC_2 H_5$)

water

ethanoic acid

ethanol A colourless, flammable **alcohol** whose **boiling point** is 78°C. Ethanol is the alcohol contained in alcoholic drinks. These are made by **fermentation**, but in the chemical industry it is made by the hydration of **ethene**:

$$C_2H_4(g) + H_2O(l) \rightarrow C_2H_5OH(l)$$

Ethanol is used in industry as a solvent and to produce **esters** and **ethers**, and to make cosmetics. It is also used in **methylated spirits**. It can be oxidized to ethanal and **ethanoic acid**, but this is now not carried out commercially.

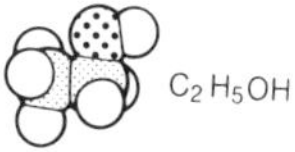

C_2H_5OH

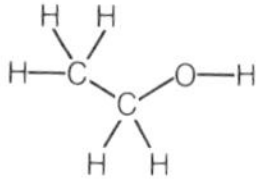

ethanol

ethene (formerly **ethylene**) A gaseous **alkene** which is produced by **cracking alkanes** (e.g. **ethane** and **naphtha**).

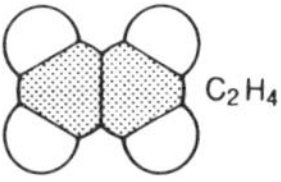

C_2H_4

(a)

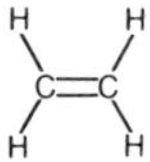

$$C_2H_4 + H_2O \rightarrow C_2H_5OH$$

$$+$$

$$H-OH$$

$$C_2H_4 + Br_2 \rightarrow C_2H_4Br_2$$

$$+$$

(b)   Br–Br

ethene (a) The compound, (b) adding molecules across its double bond to produce ethanol and ethylene dibromide.

Because it is an **unsaturated** compound it is reactive. It is a very important chemical being used to make **plastics** such as **poly(ethene)** and **poly(chloroethene)**. Ethene can add molecules across its **double bond**, e.g. to produce **ethanol**. These are addition reactions.

ethers **Organic compounds** which have an **oxygen atom** bonded to two **carbon** atoms.

One of the most important is diethyl ether (ethoxyethane). Diethyl ether is usually known simply as *ether*. This is the ether which was once widely used as an **anaesthetic** and which is today used as a solvent for substances which do not **dissolve** in **water**. It is very flammable and air/ether **mixtures** are dangerously explosive.

It is produced by the action of **concentrated sulphuric acid** on **ethanol**.

$C_4H_{10}O$

ethers diethyl ether

ethylene See **ethene**.

ethyl ethanoate The **ester** produced by reacting **ethanol** and **ethanoic acid**. It is used as a **solvent** in glues and **paints**.

ethyne (or **acetylene**) A gaseous **alkyne** which is flammable and which forms explosive **mixtures** with **air**. It can be produced by the **cracking** of **petroleum** products, although it used to be made by the action of water on calcium carbide:

$$CaO(s) + 3C(s) \rightarrow CaC_2(s) + CO(g)$$

$$CaC_2(s) + 2H_2O(l) \rightarrow C_2H_2(g) + Ca(OH)_2(s)$$

The gas was once widely used for illumination, being burnt in special lamps. They were used in mines and on bicycles. Today ethyne has largely been replaced as a feedstock for **chloroethene** and then **poly(chloroethane)** because of its cost. It is used to produce very high **temperatures** by being burnt in the oxyacetylene torch used for welding and cutting metal. Temperatures of 3000°C can be obtained if **oxygen** is used.

ethyne

eutrophic   Over-rich in nutrients. Eutrophication is caused by fertilizers and other chemicals such as **phosphates** from sewage works. These get into the **water** and cause the rapid growth of plants such as weed. The weed chokes the water and removes a lot of the **oxygen** and prevents sunlight penetrating down into the water. A lake or river is described as eutrophic if there is not enough oxygen in the water to support animal and plant life. See **pollution, acid rain.**

evaporation The process leading to a change of **state** from **liquid** to **vapour** which can occur at any **temperature** up to the **boiling point**. It takes place because **molecules** escape from the body of the liquid into the **atmosphere**. Only a small proportion of the molecules have sufficient **energy** to escape at any time but over a period they will all escape. Generally speaking, the lower the boiling point, the faster will be the rate of evaporation.

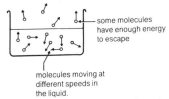

some molecules have enough energy to escape

molecules moving at different speeds in the liquid.

evaporation Molecules escaping from the body of a liquid into the atmosphere.

exothermic reaction A **reaction** in which **heat energy** is released to the surroundings from the reactants. The **bonds** of the products contain less energy than the bonds of the reactants. The products are more stable than the reactants.

Many common reactions are exothermic. All **combustion** and **neutralization** reactions are exothermic. For example:

(a) the **Haber process**

$$3H_2(g) + N_2(g) \rightarrow 2NH_3(g)$$

(b) the **contact process**

$$2SO_2(g) + O_2(g) \rightarrow 2SO_3(g)$$

are both exothermic reactions at **room temperature**. **Enthalpy** changes (ΔH) are less than zero (negative). See **endothermic reactions**, **energy changes**.

explosion A rapid expansion of **gas** which causes a shock wave. Common explosives are gunpowder, **dynamite**, nitroglycerine and TNT. These materials react with **oxygen** if *detonated* and large **temperatures** are produced. A lot of gas is also produced and the gas **molecules** and the shock wave produced by the **reaction** travel outwards from the explosion with great **energy**. It is this energy which causes the damage in explosions. In nuclear explosions the vast amount of energy locked within the **nucleus** of **atoms** is released.

faraday (F) The amount of electric charge possessed by a **mole** of **electrons** (about 96 500 **coulombs**). This amount of electricity is needed to liberate one mole of **atoms** of a *univalent* **element** (e.g. silver) during **electrolysis**:

$$Ag^+ \quad + \quad e^- \quad \rightarrow \quad Ag$$

| One mole of | One mole of | One mole of |
| silver ions. | electrons. | silver atoms. |

Named after the English physicist and chemist Michael Faraday, 1791–1867.

fats Esters of **fatty acids**. They are common constituents of food and a good source of **energy**, but there are worries that the UK diet contains too much fat. Oils are fats which are **liquid** at 20 °C.

fatty acid An **acid** with the general formula $C_nH_{2n}O_2$. These **compounds** are found in both animals and plants, combined with glycerol as **esters**. These form the oils and **fats** which are such an important part of our diet.

Fatty acids can be **saturated**, where all the carbon-carbon **bonds** are single bonds, or **unsaturated**, where some of the **carbon**-carbon bonds are double ones.

Fehling's test. A test used to detect certain **organic reducing agents**. Aldehydes can be distinguished from ketones, and **sugars** such as **glucose** from **starch** by using the test. Fehling's **solution** is a **mixture** of copper(II) sulphate, sodium hydroxide and sodium potassium tartrate. When it is heated with an appropriate reducing agent, e.g. **glucose** or ethanal, the copper(II) **salt** is reduced to a red **precipitate** of copper(I) oxide (Cu_2O).

Named after the German chemist H. C. von Fehling, 1812–85, who devised the test.

fermentation A process whereby **chemical changes** are made to **organic** chemicals by the use of living organisms such as **yeasts** and bacteria. The changes are brought about by **enzymes** acting as **catalysts**.

One important example is the changing of **sugars** to **ethanol** by the action of yeast:

$$\underset{\text{glucose}}{C_6H_{12}O_6} \quad \overset{\text{zymase}}{\rightarrow} \quad \underset{\text{ethanol}}{2C_2H_5OH} \ + \ \underset{\text{carbon dioxide}}{2CO_2}$$

This reaction is used to make alcoholic drinks:

malted barley ⟶ beer
⟶ whisky (after **fractional distillation**)

fruit, e.g. grapes ⟶ wine
⟶ sherry and port
⟶ brandy (after fractional distillation)

fertilizer A substance which is added to the soil to replace the nutrients which have been removed by plants. Fertilizers may be natural, e.g. manure and compost, or artificial, e.g. ammonium nitrate, superphosphate. **Com-**

pounds containing **nitrogen**, **phosphorus** and **potassium** (N,P,K) are the main constituents of artificial fertilizers. The addition of fertilizers to the land is an important part of the **nitrogen cycle**.

Nitrate in the soil can be washed out (*leeched*) and it can enter waterways, lakes and the like. If this happens, it can enter the public water supply where high concentrations can be harmful, especially to the young.

High **phosphate** concentrations in water lead to eutrophication, but most of the phosphate in rivers comes from sewage and effluent from washing powders rather than from fertilizers. See **superphosphate**, **eutrophic**, **pollution**.

fibre 1. A material which can be made from a yarn and used to produce fabrics by knitting or weaving. Fibres can be produced from natural materials such as **wool**, **silk**, **cotton** and linen, or from **synthetic** materials such as **nylon**, **poly(propene)** and **rayon**.

2. Bulky material from plants which swells inside the body and aids the digestion process. Fibre is an important part of our diet. Fruit and grain are good sources.

fibre glass Material made up of fine threads of **glass**. These can be formed into matting or into yarn. Fibre glass is used as an insulating material and is mixed with resins to form structures such as boats and car body panels. See **insulator**.

filter A device that allows some substances to pass through it but not others; it also means to pass something through a filter.

An insoluble **solid** and a **liquid** can be separated by pouring the **mixture** into a filter paper in a filter funnel. The liquid (or **solution**) passes through the paper. This liquid is known as the *filtrate*. The solid (known as the *residue*) is left in the filter paper. The whole process is known as *filtration*.

fire triangle A **symbol** summarizing the three things which have to be present for a fire to burn: **fuel**, heat and **oxygen**.

fire triangle

fission The process of breaking or splitting into parts. If a **molecule** is split into two or more parts it is said to undergo fission. In **nuclear**

reactions the fission of a large **atom**, e.g. **uranium** into two smaller ones, e.g. **barium** and **krypton** releases enormous amounts of **energy**.

fixing nitrogen Any process which converts atmo- spheric **nitrogen** into **compounds** which are useful as **fertilizers**. Fixing occurs in the **Haber process** and is carried out by bacteria found on the roots of certain plants, e.g. peas and beans.

flame Light and heat energy given off when substances react and hot **gases** are produced. Flames vary in their colour and their **temperature**. The gas **burner** flame when the air hole is *closed* is yellow because the flame pro-

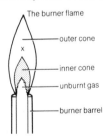

The burner flame

— outer cone

— inner cone

— unburnt gas

— burner barrel

flame Appearance of a gas burner flame when the air hole is open. X marks the hottest place.

duced contains tiny glowing particles of unburnt **carbon**. The flame when the air hole is *open* (shown in the diagram) has different parts to it. The temperature varies in the different parts of the flame.

flame test   A test used to identify **metal ions** present in **compounds**.

A clean nichrome or **platinum** wire is dipped into **concentrated hydrochloric acid** and then into a sample of the compound under test. The wire, which now has a small amount of the compound attached to it, is then put into the hottest part of the **flame**. Metals are characterized by specific colours:

Copper:	green/blue	Potassium:	lilac
Calcium:	brick red	Barium:	apple green
Sodium:	yellow/orange	Lithium:	bright red

flax   **Natural fibres** of **cellulose** which are used to make linen. Linen is a hard-wearing fabric which absorbs **water** well.

fluorine (F$_2$)   A gaseous, non-metallic **element** in **group** VII of the **periodic table**. It is a **halogen** and the most reactive element known.

Fluorine is a vigorous **oxidizing agent** which will even oxidize **chloride ion** and **water**:

$$2Cl^-(aq) + F_2(g) \rightarrow 2F^-(aq) + Cl_2(aq)$$

$$2H_2O(l) + F_2(g) \rightarrow 4HF(g) + O_2(g)$$

Compounds of **carbon** and fluorine (**CFCs**) are important refrigerants and **aerosol** propellants.

Fluorine is extracted by the **electrolysis** of a molten fluoride, e.g. KHF_2. Fluoride compounds are added to toothpaste to reduce tooth decay and uranium hexafluoride (UF_6) is used to separate uranium **isotopes**. See **poly(tetrafluoroethene)**.

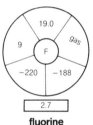

fluorine

foam A **mixture** of **gas** and **liquid** in which small bubbles of gas are separated by a thin film of the liquid. Foams will not form if the substances are **pure**, as stabilizers are needed. In ice creams and other foods where foams are used, **additives** are used to hold the foam together. Foams are used in fire-fighting because they are good at smothering the burning material and preventing flammable **vapours** from escaping.

formaldehyde See **methanal**.

formalin An **aqueous solution** of **methanal**. It is used to preserve biological specimens.

formula See **empirical formula** and **molecular formula**.

fossil fuels See **fuels**.

fractional distillation (or **fractionation**) A process of separating the components of a **mixture**. A **solvent** can be separated from a **solution** by the process of simple **distillation**. For a mixture of liquids with different **boiling points** it is usual to distil it and collect the products (*distillates*) which boil in definite **temperature** ranges. These distillates are termed *fractions*.

The exact temperature range of these fractions can be varied depending on the product which is in greatest demand. The distillation of whisky and brandy also involves fractional distillation. See **fuel**.

Frasch process A method of obtaining **sulphur** from deep underground. A double well is sunk and superheated water is passed down. This liquifies the sulphur which is then blown to the surface by compressed **air**.

Named after the German-born chemical engineer Herman Frasch, 1851–1914.

freeze-drying The removal of **water** from a frozen substance by **evaporation** at low **pressure**. This is used in the food industry to produce instant coffee and is used in industry to freeze sensitive material which might be damaged by other methods of freezing.

fructose A **sugar molecule**. Its formula is $C_6H_{12}O_6$ and it is found in Golden Syrup and honey.

fuel A substance which releases **heat energy** when it is treated in a certain way. In most fuels, the energy is released by **combustion**. Nuclear fuels, e.g. **uranium** and **plutonium**, produce heat because of changes that occur inside the atom. The **nuclear reactions** generate very large amounts of energy.

Fossil fuels	Organic fuels	Energy release
Natural gas	Wood	All burn in oxygen
Petroleum	Waste materials	to release carbon
Coal		dioxide and water
Peat		
Coke		

fuel Releasing heat energy through combustion.

fuel cell A device which converts chemical **energy** directly into electrical energy. The way it works is the reverse of **electrolysis**. Gases such as **hydrogen** (the **fuel**) and **oxygen** are passed over special porous **electrodes** and a **reaction** takes place (in this case the gases are converted into **water**). As this happens an electric **current** flows round the circuit. Fuel cells have been used in spacecraft, but commercial versions have not yet been made for use on earth.

functional group In **organic chemistry** the **atom** or group of atoms present in a molecule which is responsible for the characteristic properties of that molecule. For example:

$-CO_2H$	carboxylic acid
$-CHO$	aldehyde
$-NH_2$	amine

The 'functional groups' of organic chemistry correspond to the 'radicals' of **inorganic chemistry**. See **radical**.

fusion This means coming together and has two particular uses in chemistry.
1. Fusion is another term for melting. See **latent heat**.
2. Some **nuclear reactions** involve two **atoms** coming together to form a single atom. This is the opposite of **fission** and can involve the

release of enormous quantities of **energy**. **Hydrogen** bombs are fusion weapons. Attempts are being made to use fusion reactions to generate electricity.

(g) The **state symbol** used to denote that a substance is a **gas**:

$$CO_2(g), O_2(g), NH_3(g), H_2O(g), H_2(g)$$

galena A **mineral** form of lead(II) sulphide (PbS) which is the principle **ore** of **lead**.

galvanizing A process for coating **iron** and **steel** sheeting with a thin layer of **zinc**. This is called *galvanized iron*. Zinc is more resistant to corrosion than iron and so it can protect the **metal**. Also, if the coating is scratched and the iron and zinc come into contact with a **liquid** and an electrochemical cell is set up, the zinc reacts rather than the iron — it is more reactive. So, galvanizing protects the iron even when the protective layer is broken. See **sacrificial anode**.

gamma rays A form of high **energy** electromagnetic radiation. They are produced in **nuclear reactions** and have great penetrating powers. They are similar to **X-rays**. They are used in the treatment of cancer — they kill body cells. They are also used to sterilize substances such as surgical instruments and animal foodstuffs.

gas A **state of matter** in which **atoms** and **molecules** have few **bonds** between them and consequently have a large amount of freedom of movement. They move at high velocity and in random directions.

When **heat energy** is supplied to a **liquid**, the atoms or molecules are given increased **kinetic energy**; this may be sufficient to overcome the bonds which hold them together in the liquid state. If this happens the liquid boils and turns into a gas or **vapour**. In a gas, atoms or molecules fill the whole container and their collisions with the walls of the container exert a **pressure**.

gas laws The laws that describe the behaviour of gases. The two main ones are **Boyle's law** and **Charles' law**. If they are combined we realize that for a fixed mass of gas:

$$\frac{(\text{Pressure}) \times (\text{Volume})}{(\text{Temperature})} = \text{constant}$$

or:

$$\frac{PV}{T} = \text{constant (T is in Kelvin)}$$

This means that if we compare gases under different conditions, e.g. different **temperature** and **pressure** then:

$$\frac{P_1 V_1}{T_1} \quad = \quad \frac{P_2 V_2}{T_2} \quad = \quad \text{constant}$$

condition 1   condition 2

This allows us to obtain much useful information about gases by calculation rather than by measurement. See **STP**.

gel A colloidal **solution** which has set to form a jelly. Examples are the sweet fruit jellies which you can make at home to eat and the light-sensitive layer on photographic film. These are both based on **gelatin**.

gelatin A complex **mixture** of **amino acids** which is made by boiling animal bones, hides and cartilage in **dilute acids**. Gelatins are widely used in foods, glues and photography. See **gel**.

general formula In **organic chemistry**, a formula which shows the relative numbers of the different **atoms** in terms of the variable 'n' for all the members of a particular family of **compounds**. The actual formula of a particular compound is found by substituting for n. For example, the general formula of the **alkanes** is $C_n H_{2n+2}$.

Methane has 1 Carbon $\therefore$ n = 1 $\therefore$ formula = CH_4

Butane has 4 Carbons $\therefore$ n = 4 $\therefore$ formula = $C_4 H_{10}$

germicide   A substance which is used to reduce or prevent the growth of micro-organisms. Germicides are used both in the home to deal with minor cuts and grazes, and in hospitals during treatment of wounds and in surgery. Many modern **compounds** are based on the molecule **phenol**. Antiseptics and **disinfectants** are kinds of germicide.

giant structure   **Atoms** or **ions** that have large numbers of particles present in a **crystal lattice**. Each particle has a strong force of attraction for all the other particles which are near to it. In this way attractive forces are spread through the structure and giant structures tend to have high **melting** and **boiling points**. Ionic substances have giant structures as do most **elements**, e.g. all **metals** and several **non-metals**.

glass   A hard transparent **mixture** of silicates. The cheapest and commonest kind of glass is called *soda glass*. It is made by heating together **sand**, sodium carbonate, calcium oxide and broken glass (cullet). The hot **liquid** is cooled down very slowly. The slowness of cooling means that the glass does not crystallize. Glass is a *supercooled liquid*.

In *lead glass*, the sodium carbonate is replaced by lead(II) oxide. This gives a glass with a high refractive index. It is used in making **crystal** glassware. See **borosilicate glass, silica**.

global warming The increase in the **temperature** of the **Earth's atmosphere**. Since 1860, the temperature is estimated to have risen by 0.55°C, and the rate of increase is thought to be getting larger. The increasing amount of **greenhouse gases** in the atmosphere is thought to be the cause, although not everyone agrees.

glucose A **monosaccharide molecule**. It is found in honey, Golden Syrup and fruits. All **sugar** and **starch** which enters our bodies is converted to glucose. It is then used to provide **energy**.

gluten A **mixture** of **proteins** found in wheat. Gluten is an elastic material which stretches when bread rises.

glycol A material consisting of ethane-1, 2-diol which is used as **antifreeze** material in engines. The **compound** contains two **alcohol** (OH) groups and is made from **ethene** by **oxidation** to epoxyethane and then **water** is added to give the

glycol Oxidizing ethene to obtain glycol.

diol. Ethene is obtained by the **cracking** of **petroleum**.

gold A valuable **metal** which is prized for its use as jewellery and often used as a substitute for money. It is found uncombined with other **elements** and the major deposits are in South Africa and the USSR. Chemically it is very **inert** reacting only with vigorous **oxidizing agents** such as **chlorine** and certain **acids**, e.g. *aqua regia*. Gold is a soft metal and for most uses it is alloyed with **copper** or **silver**.

Pure gold is said to be 24-carat gold. 9-carat gold is 9 parts gold to 15 parts copper, i.e. 37.5% gold. This is hard and is commonly used in jewellery.

gold

gramme (g) A unit of **mass**. It is 1/1000 of a kilogramme and is used in all scientific work. The **symbol** 'g' is used, e.g. 100 g.

granite An **igneous** rock widely used as a building material.

graphite An allotropic form of **carbon**. It is found naturally as *plumbago*. **Charcoal** consists of small particles of graphite. It is a **giant structure** with the carbon **atoms** bonded together in a hexagonal arrangement in layers or planes.

There are strong **bonds** between the atoms in the planes but the bonds between the atoms in different planes are weak. It is possible for the planes to slip over each other.

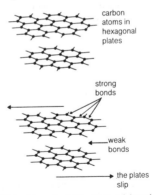

carbon atoms in hexagonal plates

strong bonds

weak bonds

the plates slip

graphite The giant structure of bonded carbon atoms.

Because of this property, graphite is very useful as a lubricant and, of course, in pencils where layers of graphite are left behind on the paper.

Graphite also finds use as *electrodes* in the extraction of elements, e.g. **sodium, aluminium** and **chlorine**, since it is an electrical **conductor**.

greenhouse effect The increase in global temperature caused by the build-up of gases in the **Earth's atmosphere** which trap beneath them the Sun's energy reflected from the Earth. This trapped energy keeps the planet 40°C warmer than it would otherwise be. In doing this it is rather like a greenhouse — hence the term — but the mechanism for warming the Earth and keeping a greenhouse hot are quite different. See **global warming, greenhouse gas**.

greenhouse gas A **gas** whose **molecules** contribute to the **greenhouse effect** and **global warming** by absorbing **energy** emitted or reflected from the surface of the Earth.

Gas	Formula	% contribution to the greenhouse effect
Carbon dioxide	CO_2	>50
Methane	CH_4	20
CFC gases	e.g. CCl_2F_2	<15
Nitrous oxide	N_2O	10
Ozone	O_3	<5

group The arrangement in the **periodic table** of the **elements**. They are arranged in horizontal **periods** and vertical groups. The elements in these groups have similar chemical properties, e.g.

Group I	lithium, sodium, potassium
Group II	beryllium, magnesium, calcium
Group III	boron, aluminium
Group IV	carbon, silicon
Group V	nitrogen, phosphorus
Group VI	oxygen, sulphur
Group VII	fluorine, chlorine, bromine
Group 0	helium, neon, argon

Each group has a characteristic **electronic configuration**: the outermost electron shell contains the same number of **electrons** for each member of the group. This is the same as the group number.

gutta-percha An **isomer** of natural **rubber**.

gypsum A **mineral** form of calcium sulphate ($CaSO_4.2H_2O$).

Haber process Process of making **ammonia** from **hydrogen** and **nitrogen**. Nitrogen is obtained from the **air** and hydrogen from the steam **reforming** of **natural gas**. Any **sulphur** is removed from the raw materials by **desulphurization** and then **steam** is added:

$$CH_4(g) + 2H_2O(g) \rightarrow CO_2(g) + 4H_2(g)$$

The carbon dioxide is removed by passing the gas through potassium carbonate solution:

$$CO_2(g) + K_2CO_3(aq) + H_2O(l) \rightarrow 2KHCO_3(aq)$$

Air is then added to give a 3:1 hydrogen:nitrogen mixture. The gases are reacted together at 500°C and 200 **atmospheres pressure**. An **iron catalyst** is used:

$$N_2(g) + 3H_2(g) \rightleftharpoons 2NH_3(g)$$

It is an **equilibrium reaction** and the conditions are chosen to produce as much ammonia as possible in the shortest time. Under these conditions about 15% of the reactants are converted to ammonia. Using a *lower* temperature will generate *more* ammonia but at a much slower **rate**. Conversely, using a *higher* temperature will produce the ammonia more quickly, but the **yield** will be lower. The chosen conditions are the *optimum* ones.

Named after the German chemist Fritz Haber, 1886–1934, who developed the process.

haematite A **mineral** form of iron(III) oxide (Fe_2O_3) which is one of the main raw materials for the production of **iron**.

haemoglobin The red pigment which is found in red blood corpuscles. It contains an **atom** of

iron in the complex **molecule**. **Oxygen** reacts with the pigment forming *oxyhaemoglobin* and oxygen is released from the complex where it is needed. **Carbon monoxide** also reacts with haemoglobin, forming *carboxyhaemoglobin*. This is a very stable compound and prevents the carriage of oxygen. This is why carbon monoxide is such a dangerous **poison**. It is important that the body obtains sufficient iron each day to maintain the correct levels of haemoglobin. The daily requirement is about 11 mg. Insufficiency leads to the condition known as *anaemia*.

half-life   The time taken for the **radioactivity** of an **isotope** to decrease to half of its original value. When a radioactive **isotope** gives off **alpha** or **beta particles** (decays) it changes into a different isotope. As the decay occurs the number of nuclei becomes fewer. The decay of an isotope is usually traced by measuring the **rate** at which particles are emitted. This rate is proportional to the number of nuclei present.

The plot in the graph opposite shows the decay of an isotope with a half-life of one minute, i.e. in each minute the number of particles emitted falls by half e.g. 4000–2000, 2000–1000, etc.

There is great variety in the length of half-lives from isotope to isotope. The half-life of any one isotope is constant, however, under all conditions of **temperature** and **pressure**.

Isotope	Half-life
Carbon-14	5730 years
Oxygen-20	14 seconds
Copper-64	756 minutes
Uranium-234	250 000 years

half-life The half-lives of different isotopes.

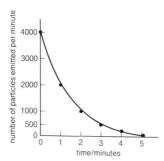

half-life The decay of an isotope with a half-life of 1 minute.

half-reaction It is often useful to represent a reaction by two half-reactions. For example, the **displacement** of **copper ions** from **solution** by **zinc**:

$$Cu^{2+}(aq) + Zn(s) \rightarrow Zn^{2+}(aq) + Cu(s)$$

can be viewed as

(a) $Cu^{2+}(aq) + 2e^- \rightarrow Cu(s)$
(b) $Zn(s) \rightarrow Zn^{2+}(aq) + 2e^-$

From these half-reactions it is easy to see that the zinc is being **oxidized** by the copper ions and that the copper ions are being reduced by the zinc. Half-reactions are particularly useful for looking at **redox** reactions.

halide A **compound** of a **halogen** with another **element**. Examples include:

hydrogen chloride (HCl)   sodium bromide (NaBr)

calcium fluoride (CaF_2)   silicon tetrachloride ($SiCl_4$)

Metal halides tend to be **ionic**, whereas non-metal halides have **covalent bonds**. Metal halides can be produced by reacting the elements together:

$$2Na(s) + Cl_2(g) \rightarrow 2NaCl(s)$$

halogens Elements in **group** VII of the **periodic table**. They are all poisonous, non-metallic elements. **Fluorine** and **chlorine** are **gases**, **bromine** is a **liquid** and **iodine** is a **solid** at room temperature. They are all **oxidizing agents**. Their oxidizing power and chemical reactivity decreases in the order:

$F_2 > Cl_2 > Br_2 > I_2$, i.e. as the group is descended.

They react vigorously with **metals** and **hydrogen** forming **halides**. They all contain seven **electrons** in the outer **shell** of the **atom** and form univalent **anions**, e.g. Cl^- Br^-.

hardboard   Material made from small chips of wood which are heated to a high temperature forming a **mass** of **cellulose** fibres. These are then heated in a press to produce hardboard which has a glossy, water-resistant surface and is used in modern furniture production.

hardening   A process in which **unsaturated oils** are reacted with **hydrogen** to produce **saturated compounds** which are more suitable for the production of vegetable oils and margarines.

hardness of water   Water that has passed over and through rocks which have dissolved in the water, e.g. **limestone, chalk** and **gypsum** ($CaSO_4$). Water from the mains supply is described as being soft or hard. Hard water does not easily lather with soap but forms a scum. It requires more soap than soft water which lathers easily. Soft water has collected in areas of the country where the rocks are insoluble in water, e.g. the granite areas such as the Lake District, Cornwall and the Highlands of Scotland.

Hardness is caused by dissolved **calcium** and **magnesium** salts. The **metal ions** are actually responsible since they chemically react with the soap forming 'scum'. There are two types of hard water: temporary and permanent

Temporary hard water contains dissolved calcium hydrogen-carbonate due to slightly acidic rain water dissolving chalk and limestone.

$$CaCO_3(s) + H_2O(l) + CO_2(g) \rightleftharpoons Ca(HCO_3)_2(aq)$$

| calcium carbonate | rainwater | calcium hydrogen carbonate |

It is called temporary since it is simply removed by boiling, which reverses the reaction to form the insoluble carbonate.

Permanent hard water contains dissolved calcium sulphate and magnesium sulphate. These are not removed by boiling. They can be removed by adding sodium carbonate to precipitate the insoluble carbonates.

Soap forms a scum with hard water because of the formation of insoluble calcium salts. Soapless **detergents** do not do this. The use of kettles and immersion heaters with hard water becomes increasingly difficult and expensive because calcium carbonate is deposited on the heating elements making them inefficient. Substances such as *calgon* and *permutit* are used to make water softer through the use of **ion exchange**.

hazard warnings   See **Appendix B**.

heat energy All substances possess heat energy. The higher their **temperature**, the more **energy** they possess. The source of this energy is the movement of atoms and molecules, i.e. their **kinetic energy**.

Heat energy is taken in during **endothermic reactions** and given out during **exothermic reactions**.

heat exchange A process where **heat energy** contained in one material is transferred to another. In industry, this takes place in *heat exchangers* and heat produced in one part of a process can be transferred to another part, thus saving energy and money. Chemical production plants are carefully designed in order to make heat exchange as efficient as possible. Heat exchange also takes place in the home. Central heating systems, freezers and fridges all use this process.

heat of combustion The **heat energy** released when one **mole** of a substance is burnt in **oxygen** (with no change in **volume**).

helium (He) Helium is a **noble gas**. It is found in **natural gas** (up to 6%) and is present in the **atmosphere** to a very small extent. It is completely unreactive and the gas is **monatomic**. It is used in airships as it is eight times less dense than air and non-flammable. Helium mixed with

oxygen is also used in breathing apparatus for deep-sea divers.

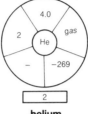

helium

heterogeneous reaction When chemical reactions occur between substances which are in different physical **states**, i.e. **gases**, **liquids** and/or **solids**, the reactions are described as heterogeneous. *Hetero* means different. Examples:

$$Zn(s) + 2HCl(aq) \rightarrow ZnCl_2(aq) + H_2(g)$$

$$2H_2O(l) + 2Na(s) \rightarrow 2NaOH(aq) + H_2(g)$$

$$2Na(s) + Cl_2(g) \rightarrow 2NaCl(s)$$

$$CuCO_3(s) \rightarrow CuO(s) + CO_2(g)$$

See **homogeneous reaction**.

homogeneous reaction **Reactions** in which all the reactants and products are in the same physical **state**. *Homo* means same. Examples include:

$$Fe(s) + S(s) \rightarrow FeS(s)$$
$$N_2(g) + 3H_2(g) \rightarrow 2NH_3(g)$$

homologous series A series of compounds with the same **general formula**. For example:

(a) **alkanes** C_nH_{2n+2}

(b) **alkenes** C_nH_{2n}.

The compounds have the same **functional groups** and have the same chemical **properties**. The physical properties of the series of compounds change only gradually.

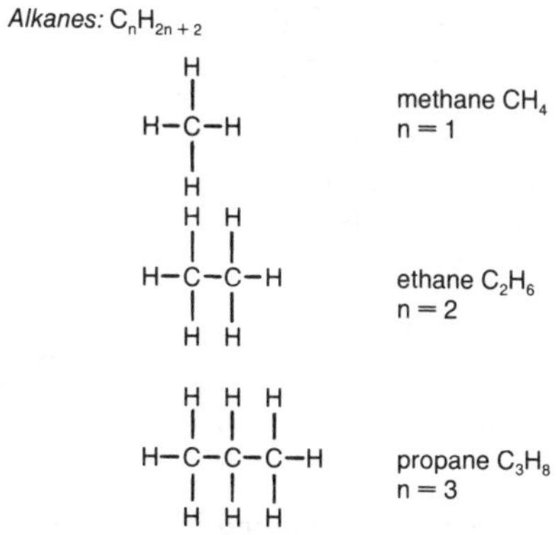

Alkanes: C_nH_{2n+2}

methane CH_4
$n = 1$

ethane C_2H_6
$n = 2$

propane C_3H_8
$n = 3$

homologous series

hydrate A **compound** which has **water** chemically combined within it. *Hydrated* **salts**, i.e. those which contain **water of crystallization** are the best examples.

$$CuSO_4.5H_2O \qquad CaCl_2.6H_2O$$

hydration A chemical **reaction** where a **compound** either reacts with a **molecule** of water to form a new substance or reacts with water to form **water of crystallization**. Examples of such reactions are:

$$C_2H_4(g) + H_2O(g) \rightarrow C_2H_6O(g)$$
ethene   water   ethanol

$$CuSO_4(s) + 5H_2O(l) \rightarrow CuSO_4.5H_2O(s)$$
anhydrous   hydrated
copper(II) sulphate   copper(II) sulphate

hydride A **compound** which contains **hydrogen** and another **element** only. Examples are:
(a) NH_3 ammonia;
(b) H_2O water;
(c) H_2S hydrogen sulphide.

The hydrides of non-metals are **covalent** compounds. Some metal hydrides contain the **ion** H^-, e.g. Na^+H^-. These compounds are very reactive and will readily decompose water.

hydrocarbon A **compound** of **hydrogen** and **carbon** only is a hydrocarbon, e.g. **alkanes**, **alkenes**, **alkynes**:
(a) CH_4 methane;

(b) C_2H_2 ethyne;

(c) C_2H_4 ethene;

(d) C_6H_6, benzene.

hydrochloric acid (HCl(aq)) A **solution** of **hydrogen chloride** in **water**; it contains **chloride** and **oxonium ions**. The maximum **concentration** of the solution is 36% (about 11 mol/dm^3). The **acid** is **monobasic** and produces **salts** called **chlorides**, e.g.

$$Fe(s) + 2HCl(aq) \rightarrow FeCl_2(aq) + H_2(g)$$

$$Mg(s) + 2HCl(aq) \rightarrow MgCl_2(aq) + H_2(g)$$

It is a **strong acid** being fully dissociated into $Cl^-(aq)$ and $H_3O^+(aq)$ ions in dilute solution. It releases **carbon dioxide** from **carbonates** and **hydrogencarbonates** and can be oxidized to **chlorine**:

$$MnO_2(s) + 4HCl(aq) \rightarrow$$

$$MnCl_2(aq) + 2H_2O(l) + Cl_2(g)$$

hydrogen (H_2) A gaseous **diatomic element**. The **atom** consists of one **proton** and one **electron**. The **isotope deuterium** contains a **neutron** in the nucleus of the atom. There is a further isotope called *tritium* which has two neutrons in its nucleus and is radioactive.

Hydrogen is very reactive. It can form **covalent bonds** by sharing electrons. For example:

$$2H_2(g) + O_2(g) \rightarrow 2H_2O(g)$$

$$C_2H_4(g) + H_2(g) \rightarrow C_2H_6(g) \; (hydrogenation)$$

Two hydrogen ions can be produced by losing the electron to form H^+ or by gaining an electron to form H^- (present in some **hydrides**). The positive hydrogen ion (H^+) is such a small, reactive species (it is a lone proton) that it does not exist alone in **solution**. In **aqueous solution** it reacts with the **water** to form the **oxonium ion**. **Acids** contain the oxonium ion.

Hydrogen is a **reducing agent**. It is used to make **methanol** and **nylon** and is growing in importance as a fuel. It is used to convert vegetable oils into *margarine*. Large quantities are used in the **Haber process**. Industrially, the gas is made from **petroleum** by the **steam** reformation of **naphtha** and **natural gas**.

In the laboratory, the gas is made by reacting a **metal** with an acid other than nitric acid, e.g.:

$$Zn(s) + 2HCl(aq) \rightarrow ZnCl_2(aq) + H_2(g)$$

It is also released by the electrolysis of aqueous solutions which contain ions of elements above hydrogen in the electrochemical series, e.g. $NaCl(aq)$, $Mg(NO_3)_2(aq)$, and by the reaction of water with alkali and alkaline earth metals, e.g. sodium, calcium.

Hydrogen is a flammable gas which causes explosive mixtures with oxygen. Great care must be taken in its preparation, collection and use.

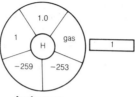

hydrogen

hydrogen bond A weak chemical **bond** formed
between **hydrogen** atoms and **atoms** of **oxygen**
or **nitrogen**. Although weaker than **covalent** or
ionic bonds, hydrogen bonds affect the physical
properties of **compounds**. **Molecules** in **water**
and **ice** are extensively hydrogen-bonded to each
other.

hydrogen bond Molecules in water and
ice.

hydrogenation In this process an **unsaturated**

compound is turned into a **saturated** one by the addition of **hydrogen**. A **catalyst** such as **nickel** is used. For example:

This process is sometimes known as **hardening**.

hydrogencarbonates (HCO$_3^-$) The **acid salts** of *carbonic acid* H_2CO_3. The best known examples are:

(a) *Sodium hydrogencarbonate* NaHCO$_3$. This is the familiar household chemical *bicarbonate of soda*. It is found in self-raising flour and **baking powder**.

(b) Calcium hydrogencarbonate Ca(HCO$_3$)$_2$. This is found in **hard water** because rainwater passes over **carbonate** rocks such as **limestone**:

$$CaCO_3(s) + CO_2(aq) + H_2O(l) \rightarrow Ca(HCO_3)_2(aq)$$

hydrogen chloride (HCl) A colourless **gas** which is very **soluble** in **water**. An **aqueous solution** is called **hydrochloric acid**. The gas can be made by reacting the **elements** together treating **sodium chloride** with concentrated **sulphuric acid**:

$$H_2(g) + Cl_2(g) \rightarrow 2HCl(g)$$

$$NaCl(s) + H_2SO_4(l) \rightarrow NaHSO_4(s) + HCl(g)$$

The gas will react with **ammonia** to form dense white fumes of **ammonium chloride**:

$$NH_3(g) + HCl(g) \rightarrow NH_4Cl(s)$$

The bonding in hydrogen chloride is **covalent** but **ions** are formed when it dissolves in a **polar solvent**, e.g. water.

hydrogen halides These are gaseous **compounds** formed between **hydrogen** and the **halogens**. They are **covalent** compounds which readily dissolve in **water** to form an acidic solution which contains the **halide ion**, e.g.

$$HBr(g) + H_2O(l) \rightarrow H_3O^+(aq) + Br^-(aq)$$

Hydrogen fluoride	HF
Hydrogen chloride	HCl
Hydrogen bromide	HBr
Hydrogen iodide	HI

hydrogen ion A positively charged **proton**:

$$H \rightarrow H^+ + e^-$$

This is such a small particle that it is very reactive. In solution, it is chemically combined with the solvent molecules. In water this is represented by the **oxonium ion**:

$$H^+ + H_2O \rightarrow H_3O^+ \quad \left[\begin{array}{c} H \quad\quad H \\ \diagdown \quad \diagup \\ O \\ | \\ H \end{array} \right]^+ \quad \text{oxonium ion}$$

The concentration of hydrogen ions in an **aqueous solution** is expressed in **pH** units, and gives a measure of the degree of acidity of the solution. See **hydroxide ion**.

hydrogen peroxide (H_2O_2) A compound is usually used as an **aqueous** solution. It readily decomposes to give **oxygen**:

$$2H_2O_2(aq) \rightarrow 2H_2O(l) + O_2(g)$$

A manganese(IV) oxide **catalyst** speeds up the reaction. It is used as a **disinfectant** and **bleach** in the home and is a powerful **oxidizing agent**. It bleaches hair to a blonde colour, and is used in industry for bleaching paper pulp and natural fibres. It is less destructive than the more powerful bleach **chlorine**.

hydrogen sulphide (H_2S) A colourless **gas** with a sweetish, sickly odour which reminds you of rotten eggs. The gas is produced when **organic** matter containing **sulphur** rots. It is often found associated with **petroleum**. It is made in the laboratory by the action of an **acid** on a **metal** sulphide, e.g.:

$$FeS(s) + 2HCl(aq) \rightarrow FeCl_2(aq) + H_2S(g)$$

The gas is *very* poisonous. Like hydrogen cyanide [HCN] it prevents the transmission of **energy** within the body. The gas can be detected by the fact that it turns a piece of filter paper soaked in a lead(II) salt to a black colour. This is because insoluble lead(II) sulphide is formed:

$$Pb^{2+}(aq) + H_2S(g) \rightarrow PbS(s) + 2H^+(aq)$$
$$\text{black}$$

A **solution** of hydrogen sulphide in water is a **weak acid** and the gas is a **reducing agent**.

hydrolysis The term for the **decomposition** of a substance by the action of **water**. The water is also decomposed. **Esters** are hydrolysed as the example shows:

ethyl ethanoate   water   **ethanoic**   **ethanol**
                                acid

hydrophilic Water-loving. The term is used to describe parts of **molecules** which readily dissolve in **water**, e.g. the ionic end of a **detergent** molecule is hydrophilic. This *attraction* for water is why detergents work. The other end of the molecule is water-hating or **hydrophobic**.

The hydrophobic part of a molecule does not dissolve in water and is not attracted to water. In a detergent this end of the molecule **bonds** with grease or oils in the material being cleaned. See **soap, detergent**.

hydrophobic   See **hydrophilic**.

hydroxide ion (OH⁻)   An **ion** found in all **alkalis**, e.g. sodium hydroxide, and in **alkaline solutions**. It is present in *all* **aqueous solutions** because of the **dissociation** of **water**:

$$H_2O \rightleftharpoons H^+ + OH^-$$

Solutions with more hydroxide ions than hydrogen ions are described as alkaline and have a **pH** greater than 7. Group I hydroxides are soluble in water. Some other hydroxides are sparingly soluble, e.g. $Mg(OH)_2$, $Ca(OH)_2$. Insoluble hydroxides can be precipitated by the use of a soluble hydroxide. For example:

$$Pb(NO_3)_2(aq) + 2NaOH(aq) \rightarrow$$

$$Pb(OH)_2(s) + 2NaNO_3(aq)$$

hygroscopic   Describes a substance which can take in up to 70% of its own **mass** of **water** without dissolving or getting wet. Examples are

copper(II) oxide, sodium chloride and **silica gel**.
See **deliquescence**.

ice Solid, crystalline **water**. Its **melting point**
at a **pressure** of 1 **atmosphere** is 0°C. The
regular, crystalline structure means that frozen
water can take on the patterns that we see in
snowflakes. Ice is less dense than water and it
floats. See **crystal**.

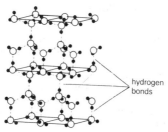

hydrogen
bonds

ice The crystalline structure of frozen
water.

igneous rocks Rocks formed when molten rock
(*magma*) cools and solidifies. Igneous rocks are
crystalline, normally contain **minerals** and
make up 90% of the earth's crust. Examples are
granite, gabbro and basalt. See **crystallization**,
rock cycle.

immiscible Not capable of being mixed. When

two **liquids** do not mix together but form two layers, one liquid on top of the other, they are described as immiscible.

One liquid will probably be **polar**, e.g. **water**, and the other non-polar, e.g. **ether**. Two polar liquids will mix completely, e.g. water and ethanol, as will two non-polar liquids, e.g. ether and **tetrachloromethane**. Two immiscible liquids may be separated using a separating funnel. See **miscible liquids**.

indicator   A substance which changes its colour under different conditions, e.g. **litmus** is red in **acid** solution and blue in **alkaline**. It can be used to indicate the **end point** of a **reaction**. Indicators are useful in **acid-base titrations** where they have different colours at different **pHs**. They are also used in titrations between **metal ions** and **complex** ions. See **universal indicator**.

inert   Unreactive. See **CFCs, noble gases**.

inert gases   See **noble gases**.

infra-red (i.r.) radiation   Invisible electromagnetic radiation with an **energy** slightly lower than that of visible radiation. i.r. radiation is produced by warm objects. Our skins are sensitive to this radiation which we experience as **heat**. Photographic film can be made which is sensitive to i.r. radiation and can be used where there is not enough visible light to take normal photographs.

inhibitor A substance which will slow down or stop a chemical **reaction**.

initiator A substance which is used to start off a chemical **reaction** such as a **polymerization** or an **explosion**.

inorganic Inorganic substances are those which do not form part of living things and have no life, for example rocks and water.

inorganic chemistry The chemistry of all the elements other than carbon. It is concerned with non-organic aspects of chemistry, i.e. **elements** and their **compounds**. This includes **carbon** the element, its **oxides**, metal **carbonates** and **hydrogencarbonates**, but excludes all organic compounds, e.g. **alcohols**, **esters**, **ethers**, **hydrocarbons**, etc. See **organic chemistry**.

insecticide See **biocide**.

insoluble Used to describe a substance which does not **dissolve** in a **solvent**.

insulator A substance which is a poor **conductor** of either **heat** or electricity.

Non-metallic elements are usually insulators, as are most **solid** compounds and **polymers**.

Graphite is an exception. Examples of efficient insulators are:

(a) Expanded **polystyrene**;

(b) **Rubber**;

(c) **Mineral wools**, e.g. *rockwool*;

(d) **Glass fibre**.

iodides Compounds of **iodine** and another **element**. For example, potassium iodide KI; hydrogen iodide HI.

iodine (I_2) A shiny, grey **non-metal**. It is a **halogen** and has a **diatomic** molecular **structure**.

Iodine is extracted from sodium iodate(v) [$NaIO_3$] and a small amount from seaweed. It is used to produce animal feeds, **catalysts**, printing inks, **dyes** and pharmaceuticals.

Silver iodide is used in photographic emulsions. The human body needs 0.07 mg of iodine per day. Its principal use in the body is in the

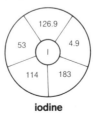

iodine

production of the hormone *thyroxine*. Potassium iodide is often added to table salt to provide this iodine.

Iodine will react with some **metals** directly to form **iodides**. It will react with **hydrogen** and **chlorine** forming [HI] and [ICl]. The **vapour** of the **element** is purple, choking and **caustic**.

ion   An **atom** or group of atoms which possess an electrical charge. When an atom gains or loses an **electron** it becomes an **ion**. **Cations** have a positive charge, **anions** have a negative charge, e.g. sodium Na^+, oxide O^{2-}. Atoms tend to gain or lose **electrons** to produce an ion with a **noble-gas** configuration. Groups of atoms (radicals) can also possess a charge. For example:

Sulphate SO_4^{2-}, Nitrate NO_3^-,
Hydroxide OH^-, Ammonium NH_4^+

They are also regarded as ions.

ion exchange   The exchange of ions of the same electrical charge between a solution and a solid in contact with it. It is possible to purify water using ion exchange by passing it over a resin (called an *ion exchange resin*) in a tube. With sea-water the **sodium ions** would be replaced by **hydrogen** ions and the **chloride** ions by **hydroxide** ions. In other words, sodium chloride would be *exchanged* for water. The ions are bonded to the resin and exchange occurs. The product is *de-ionized* water. This method can be used for softening water, e.g. **calcium** ions are replaced by **sodium** ions.

ionic bonds Chemical **bonds** which occur because of the electrostatic attractive forces between negatively and positively charged **ions**.

Ionic bonds occur in **compounds** of **non-metals** from groups VI and VII and metallic **elements**, e.g.:

$$Na^+Cl^-   \quad Mg^{2+}Br_2^-$$

and also in compounds involving **radicals** such as sulphate and nitrate, e.g.:

$$Cu^{2+}SO_4^{2-} \text{ and } K^+NO_3^-$$

Ionic compounds have **giant structures**.

ionic equation An **equation** that shows only those **ions** that take part in a **reaction**. For example, the reaction between sodium hydroxide and hydrochloric acid can be described by the molecular **equation**:

$$NaOH(aq) + HCl(aq) \rightarrow NaCl(aq) + H_2O(l)$$

This reaction is an ionic one and can be represented in an *ionic* form:

$$Na^+OH^-(aq) + H^+Cl^-(aq) \rightarrow$$
$$Na^+Cl^-(aq) + H_2O(l)$$

Because Na^+ and Cl^- appears on *both* sides of the equation they do not take any part in the reaction and can be omitted. The ionic equation is therefore:

$$OH^-(aq) + H^+(aq) \rightarrow H_2O(l)$$

The other ions are **spectator ions**.

ionization The process by which an **atom** loses or gains **electrons** and becomes an **ion**.

ionizing radiation Radiation which can cause changes in living material. There are different types of radiation, and each type penetrates materials to a different extent. Ionizing radiation is used in medicine for both diagnosis and treatment. See **radioactivity**.

iron The most widely used metallic **element**. It is mainly encountered in **steel alloys** and in this form it is used for building girders, machine bodies (cars, cookers, fridges), containers (boxes, cans, drums), tools, utensils and many other items of everyday life. The metal is extracted from ores such as haematite (Fe_2O_3) and magnetite (Fe_3O_4) by reduction with **carbon monoxide** in the **blast furnace**. The **ion** which is produced in this way is brittle and is made into many different kinds of steel to strengthen it and to give it special properties.

One of the main problems with iron is that it rusts, i.e. it oxidizes in air to produce a soft, crumbly oxide.

$$\underset{\substack{\text{(strong, useful}\\\text{metal)}}}{\text{Iron}} \xrightarrow{\text{(moist air)}} \underset{\substack{\text{(weak, worthless}\\\text{oxide)}}}{\text{Iron(III) oxide (Fe}_2\text{O}_3\text{)}}$$

Iron is a **transition metal** and can have **valency** of 2 or 3. The metal reacts with dilute **acids** to form iron(II) **compounds**, e.g.:

$$Fe(s) + 2HCl(aq) \rightarrow FeCl_2(aq) + H_2(g)$$

but will give iron(III) compounds when reacted with vigorous **oxidizing agents** such as **chlorine**:

$$2Fe(s) + 3Cl_2(g) \rightarrow 2FeCl_3(s)$$

Iron has a **reversible reaction** with **steam**:

$$3Fe(s) + 4H_2O(g) \rightleftharpoons Fe_3O_4(s) + 4H_2(g)$$

Iron(III) compounds can be identified by their giving a red colour with potassium thiocyanate solution (KCNS). Iron(II) compounds do not do this but do produce a blue colour with a **solution** of potassium hexacyanoferrate(III) $K_3Fe(CN)_6$.

Furthermore, when reacted with sodium hydroxide solution, iron(II) solutions produce a muddy green **precipitate**, whereas iron(III) solutions produce a rust-brown precipitate. See **steel manufacture**.

iron

iron compounds

Iron(III) oxide Fe_2O_3 (haematite)	A yellowish/brown pigment used in the paper, linoleum and ceramics industries. It is used as a **catalyst** and as a polish, e.g. in jeweller's rouge.
Iron(III) chloride $FeCl_3$	Produced by reacting the elements together. It is an important **catalyst** and also finds use in the purification of water and in the production of pharmaceutical products.
Iron(II) sulphate $FeSO_4.7H_2O$	Iron(II) sulphate can be recovered from the waste materials left behind in the **electroplating** processes. It is an important compound, used in the

preservation of wood, in inks and in lithography.

Iron forms compounds with **valency** (II) and (III). Iron(II) compounds tend to be green in colour whilst iron(III) compounds are yellow or brown.

isomers Two or more different **compounds** which have the same **molecular formula**. Because the compounds are different, they have different **properties**.

ethanol   methoxymethane

isomer Ethanol and methoxymethane have the same molecular formula (C_2H_6O) but different properties.

isotopes **Atoms** of the same **element** containing different numbers of **neutrons**. Atoms of an element always contain the same number of **protons** (same **atomic number**). The number of neutrons in atoms of an element can be different (different **mass number**).

A sample of **chlorine** contains atoms which have 18 neutrons (76% of the total) and atoms which have 20 neutrons (24%). Thus, chlorine is said to have two isotopes:

$$^{35}_{17}Cl \quad ^{37}_{17}Cl$$

The ratio of the isotopes is always constant. Most elements are found in isotopic forms. Examples include:

	Istotopes	
Bromine	$^{79}_{35}Br$ (51%)	$^{81}_{35}Br$ (49%)
Carbon	$^{12}_{6}C$ (99%)	$^{13}_{6}C$ (1%)
Copper	$^{63}_{29}Cu$ (69%)	$^{65}_{29}Cu$ (31%)
Magnesium	$^{24}_{12}Mg$ (79%)	$^{25}_{12}Mg$ (10%)
	$^{26}_{12}Mg$ (11%)	

All the ones quoted are *stable* isotopes. However, many more unstable, radioactive isotopes exist. A few elements have no isotopes, i.e. they have no variation in the number of neutrons that are found in the atom. These include: **fluorine, gold, iodine, manganese, phosphorus, scandium**.

The existence of isotopes accounts for the fact that many elements have a **relative atomic mass** which is not close to a whole number, e.g. Cl=35.5.

joule   The **SI unit** of **energy** and work. It has the **symbol J**. In scientific usage the **kilojoule** (kJ) is common.

Kelvin temperature scale   The Kelvin is the **SI**

unit of **temperature**. The Kelvin (K) is the same as one degree **Celsius**. Absolute zero is 0 K.

Kelvin	0	273	310	373	K
Celsius	−273	0	37	100	°C
	absolute zero	freezing point of water	blood heat	boiling point of water	

Kelvin temperature scale   A comparison with the Celsius scale.

Note: A temperature in Kelvin does not include a degree sign (°), thus the **boiling point** of water is simply 373 K.

Named after the Scottish physicist William Thomson Kelvin, 1824–1907, famous for his work in thermodynamics and electricity.

kerosine   A product of **petroleum** refining. Its uses include **fuel** for jet aircraft and also household paraffin which can be used for heating and lighting. Kerosines boil between 160 °C and 250 °C.

kilo-   A prefix which means one thousand. In common usage, a kilo has come to mean a kilogramme, e.g. 'a kilo of potatoes'. This is imprecise and should not be used in scientific work. Examples of use:

kilogramme = 1000 g   kilometre = 1000 m

kilojoule (kJ) One thousand **joules**.

kinetic energy The **energy** a body possesses because of its motion. The greater its *velocity* (speed) the more energy it has. The kinetic energy of a particle is $\frac{1}{2}mv^2$ where m is its **mass** and v its velocity. If the mass is measured in kilogrammes and the velocity in metres/second the kinetic energy is measured in **joules**.

kinetic theory The theory that all particles (**atoms** and **molecules**) are moving and that the extent to which movement can occur depends on the **temperature**. In **solids** and **liquids** the amount of movement is restricted by **bonds** between adjacent particles. In **gases** the movement is only restricted by the walls of the container. The higher the temperature, the greater the **kinetic energy** the particles possess. See **lattice**, **change of state**.

krypton A **noble gas**. It is found in the **atmosphere** to a small extent and is used in electronic valves and fluorescent tubes. Like all noble gases, krypton is **monatomic** (see overleaf).

l 1. A **state symbol** denoting a **liquid**, e.g. $H_2O(l)$, $Hg(l)$, $H_2SO_4(l)$.
2. The unit of volume (litre) which is equivalent to $1\,dm^3$ or 1000 ml.

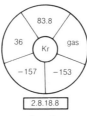

krypton

L   The symbol for the **Avogadro constant**. It is the number of particles in one **mole** of a substance. Its value is 6×10^{23} particles per mole.

lactose   A **sugar** found in all animal milk. It is a **disaccharide** with the **formula** $C_{12}H_{22}O_{11}$.

laminated   A term used to describe materials which are made up of layers of material bonded together in some way, usually with a resin. Lamination makes objects strong and flexible.

latent heat   The amount of **heat energy** released or absorbed in a **change of state** at a fixed **temperature** (e.g. **melting point** and **boiling point**). The latent heat of **fusion** is that energy needed to turn one **mole** of **solid** into a **liquid** *at its melting point*.

Similarly, the latent heat of *vaporization* is that energy required to turn one mole of liquid into a **gas** at its boiling point. These symbols can be used:

ΔH_m m=melting ΔH_b b=boiling
   (fusion)   (vaporization)

Examples:

Water	$\Delta H_m=$	6 kJ/mole
	$\Delta H_b=$	41 kJ/mole
Magnesium	$\Delta H_m=$	9 kJ/mole
	$\Delta H_b=$	129 kJ/mole

lattice A regular arrangement of **molecules**, **atoms** or **ions** within a crystalline **solid**. Lattices contain large numbers of particles which are arranged in very particular ways. See **crystal**.

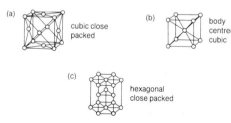

(a) cubic close packed

(b) body centred cubic

(c) hexagonal close packed

lattice Small sections of three lattices: (a) aluminium, (b) sodium, (c) magnesium.

law of constant composition   A chemical **compound** always contains the same **elements** combined in the same proportions by **mass**. Examples include the following:

(a) **Water** always has **hydrogen** and **oxygen** within it in the proportion: $^H/_O = ^2/_{16} = ^1/_8$ by mass.

(b) **Carbon dioxide** always has **carbon** and oxygen within it in the proportion: $^C/_O = ^{12}/_{32} = ^3/_8$ by mass.

law of multiple proportions   If two **elements** form more than one **compound** then there is a simple relationship between the masses of one of the elements and a fixed **mass** of the other element. In oxides of nitrogen, for example, there is a simple and steady increase in the ratio of **oxygen** to **nitrogen**.

Formula	Ratio	Simple ratio
	N:O (by mass)	N:O
N_2O	28:16	14:8
NO	14:16	14:16
NO_2	14:32	14:32
N_2O_5	28:80	14:40

law of multiple proportions   Ratios between oxides of nitrogen.

lead   A dense metallic **element** which is in

group IV of the **periodic table**. It is a soft, **mal-leable**, grey element which is extracted from galena (PbS) but 40% of the lead now produced is recycled from scrap. Lead and its **alloys** are widely used, e.g. in the lead-acid **accumulator**, solders, as protection from moisture (used around cables and on roofs), radioactive **isotopes** and **X-rays**. It is also used to make petrol **additives**, although the increasing use of **unleaded** fuel is reducing this use. Because of its chemical inert-ness, lead can be used to store **sulphuric acid**.

lead

lead compounds

Lead(II) nitrate Pb(NO₃)₂	The only common **soluble** lead compound.
Lead(II) oxide PbO	The yellow oxide, litharge. It is used in the making of **glass** and **enamels**.
Lead(IV) oxide PbO₂	Oxide is formed in the lead-acid **accumulator**.

Tetraethyl lead $Pb(C_2H_5)_4$	The **'antiknock'** agent added to **petrol** to make car engines run smoother. It is also a source of air **pollution** from car exhausts.

Lead forms lead(II) and lead(IV) **compounds**. Most lead compounds are cumulative **poisons**.

Le Chatelier's principle If a reaction is at **equilibrium** and any of the conditions are changed, further reaction will occur to counter the changes and re-establish equilibrium. For example; in the **Haber process**:

$$N_2(g) + 3H_2(g) \rightleftharpoons 2NH_3(g)$$

If extra **nitrogen** or **hydrogen** is added to an equilibrium **mixture** then more **ammonia** will be formed and the equilibrium will be re-established. Similarly, if extra ammonia is added, more nitrogen and hydrogen will be formed.

If the **pressure is** *increased* more ammonia will be formed. This is because forming more ammonia leads to a *lowering* of the pressure owing to an overall reduction in the number of gas molecules present. In this way equilibrium is re-established.

A change of **temperature** leads to a change in the proportions of the equilibrium mixture. For **exothermic** reactions (e.g. Haber process) *rais-*

ing the temperature favours the *right→left* reaction (ammonia would react to form more nitrogen and hydrogen). This is because the *right→left* reaction is **endothermic**. It therefore counters the rise in temperature by absorbing heat.

Named after the French chemist Henri Le Chatelier, 1850–1936.

lime (or quicklime) Another name for **calcium oxide**, produced by heating **limestone** above 900°C. The reaction is **endothermic**:

$$CaCO_3(s) \rightarrow CaO(s) + CO_2(g)$$

This is an important industrial chemical which is used in:

(a) **Metal** production;
(b) **Refractory** materials;
(c) **Fertilizers**;
(d) Production of other chemicals;
(e) Building materials.

It is used to make **slaked lime** and is responsible for turning impurities in the **blast furnace** into **slag**. In the laboratory it is a useful drying agent for **ammonia**.

limestone A commonly found rock which contains between 50% and 90% **calcium carbonate** ($CaCO_3$). It is used to make **lime** and **cement** and is used as building stone and hard core for foundations. See **chalk**.

limewater A dilute **solution** of the sparingly **soluble** compound **calcium hydroxide**. It is an **alkali** and is used to test for **carbon dioxide**:

$$Ca(OH)_2(aq) + CO_2(g) \rightarrow CaCO_3(s) + H_2O(l)$$

A white **precipitate** is formed seen as a milkiness in the solution. If excess carbon dioxide is bubbled through, the precipitate reacts to form the soluble **salt, calcium hydrogencarbonate**, and the **liquid** goes clear:

$$CaCO_3(s) + H_2O(l) + CO_2(g) \rightarrow Ca(HCO_3)_2(aq)$$

linear molecules Molecules which are *straight*, i.e. their **atoms** are in a line. All **molecules** which contain only two atoms must be linear but some examples of more complicated molecules are shown here:

carbon dioxide	ethyne	beryllium chloride
$O=C=O$	$H-C\equiv C-H$	$Cl-Be-Cl$

liquid A **state of matter** in which particles are loosely bonded by intermolecular forces. A liquid always takes up the shape of its container. The particles in the liquid are not fixed in a rigid framework (**lattice**). See **evaporation, boiling**.

lithium A **group I metal**. It is the least reactive **element** in the group. Nevertheless it is stored under **oil** because of its reactivity towards **air** and **water**. It is soft, and can be cut with a knife, revealing a silvery surface which tarnishes readily. It has a steady reaction with water but reacts vigorously with **acids**.

$$2Li(s) + 2H_2O(l) \rightarrow 2LiOH(aq) + H_2(g)$$

It is possible that the metal will be very important in the future if electricity can be generated by **nuclear fusion** reactions. The metal ion gives a red **flame test**.

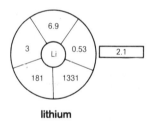

lithium

litmus A substance extracted from lichen that is used as an **acid-base indicator**; according to the **pH** scale:

acidic solution	pH 7	alkaline solution
red	purple	blue

litre The unit of liquid volume where 1 litre = 1000 cm^3. The litre is commonly used in everyday life, e.g. for fruit juice or paint. However, in scientific uses, the cubic decimetre is used instead (1000 cm^3 = 1 **dm**^{3}).

lone pair of electrons Pairs of outer **shell electrons** which are not used in **bonds** within the **compound**. They can, however, be used for forming bonds with other compounds, as the example shows.

lone pair of electrons A lone pair bonding to form an **ammonium ion**.

M see molarity.

M$_r$ The **symbol** for the **relative molecular mass** of a **compound** or **molecule**. It can be calculated by adding together the **relative atomic masses (A$_r$)** of each atom within the molecule. For example:

M$_r$ carbon monoxide (CO) = 12 + 16 = 28
M$_r$ water (H$_2$O) = (2×1) + 16 = 18

macromolecule A large **molecule**. It is usually used to describe molecules with an M_r value greater than 1000, namely, **polymers** such as the **carbohydrates** and the **plastics**, e.g. **poly(ethene)**, and molecules such as **proteins** and nucleic acids.

magnesium A shiny grey **group II metal**. It is quite reactive giving vigorous **reactions** towards **acids**. It burns vigorously in air with a bright white light, hence its use in flares, fireworks and flash bulbs. It also burns in **carbon dioxide gas**, and will react with **steam** to release **hydrogen**. The metal is obtained by the **electrolysis** of molten magnesium chloride. Much of this is extracted from seawater.

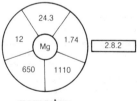

magnesium

The chief use of magnesium is in the production of low density **alloys** for use in the aircraft industry. There is no production of the metal in the UK. Much of the European production takes place in Norway because of the availability of hydroelectricity. Magnesium is also used in the production of **steel**, as a **reducing agent** in the chemical industry, and as **sacrificial anodes** in the protection of other metals.

magnesium compounds

Magnesium hydroxide $Mg(OH)_2$	Obtained by treating seawater with calcium hydroxide. It is used in pharmaceutical products such as *Milk of Magnesia* as a treatment for excess acidity in the stomach.
Magnesium carbonate $MgCO_3$	Found naturally as magnesite and as **dolomite** ($MgCO_3.CaCO_3$) and is used for making heat-resistant (refractory) materials.
Magnesium oxide MgO	Important refractory compound made by heating the carbonate.
Magnesium chloride $MgCl_2$	After extraction from seawater the molten **compound** is electrolysed to produce magnesium metal.
Magnesium sulphate $MgSO_4.7H_2O$	*Epsom Salts*. These **crystals** are used to treat constipation. They are also used as a fire-proofing agent.

malachite A hydrated **mineral** form of copper(II) carbonate. Its formula can either be written as: $Cu_2(OH)_2CO_3$ or $CuCO_3.Cu(OH)_2$.

malleable Able to be beaten or hammered into different shapes. The larger the **crystals** in a substance, the more malleable it is. Materials which are malleable are usually also **ductile**. **Metals** and **alloys** have these properties. See **annealing**.

maltose ($C_{12}H_{22}O_{11}$) This is a **disaccharide molecule**. It is found as a breakdown product of **starch**. Maltose is a **glucose dimer**.

manganese A **transition metal**. It is found naturally as the oxide (MnO_2) and is extracted either by **electrolysis** of the sulphate or by a **thermit reaction**. The chief use of the metal is in **alloys**, e.g. **steels** and **bronzes**.

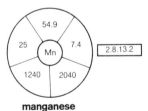

manganese

manganese compounds

Manganese(IV) oxide MnO_2	Important use in the dry **battery**. It is used as a **catalyst** and **oxidizing agent**.

| Potassium manganate(VII) KMnO$_4$ | A vivid purple crystalline substance which is a vigorous oxidizing agent. It is used as an antiseptic. It gives the MnO$_4^-$ **ion**. |

Manganese forms compounds where the metal has valency 2, 3, 4, 6 and 7. The most important ones are 2, 4 and 7.

marble A crystalline **mineral** form of **calcium carbonate** (CaCO$_3$). It is widely used as a decorative wall covering in buildings, and as a flooring material.

mass The amount of material a substance possesses. It is usually measured in grammes (g) or kilogrammes (kg).

mass number (A) In an **isotope**, the sum of the number of **protons** and **neutrons** in the **nucleus** of the **atom**. This number is shown at the top left-hand side of the **symbol** when describing the isotope (the number below it being the atomic number). For example:

$$_1^1H \quad _6^{12}C \quad _{11}^{23}Na \quad _{20}^{40}Ca \quad _{82}^{208}Pb \quad _{92}^{238}U$$

matches Small, thin sticks of wood that produce a **flame** when struck against a rough surface. The **reaction** is between **phosphorus** sulphide and **potassium** chlorate (KClO$_4$). These two chemicals are normally combined together in the match head, and when pulled across a rough surface (as on the match box), the **activation energy** is provided for the chemical reaction. This generates a lot of **heat** and a flame is produced. In *safety matches* only one chemical is contained in the match head; the other (the phosphorus sulphide) is on the side of the box. In this way, the matches cannot be lit accidentally.

melamine A colourless, crystalline compound produced from **urea**. It undergoes **condensation polymerization** with **methanal** to produce melamine resins. These are heat- and light-resistant, colourless and shatter-resistant. They are widely used as picnic-ware and as kitchen worktops.

melamine

melting A **solid** melts to form a **liquid** when the **energy** of the particles is sufficient to break up the **bonds** holding them in a **lattice**. For a **pure** substance, melting occurs at a fixed

temperature — the **melting point**. Some bonds remain but clusters of particles are mobile.

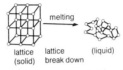

lattice   lattice   (liquid)
(solid)   break down

melting Particles of a solid breaking up to form a liquid.

melting point The **temperature** at which a **solid** melts to form a **liquid** (or a liquid solidifies to form a solid). More precisely, it is the **temperature** at which solid and liquid forms of the same substance (e.g. **ice/water**) are in **equilibrium**. At constant **pressure**, the melting point is a constant for a **pure** substance but it is *lowered* if impurities are added, hence ice can melt when sprinkled with **salt**.

mercury The only **metal** which is **liquid** at **room temperature**. It is used to make **amalgams**, in **electrolysis** cells as a **cathode**, and in thermometers. Its **compounds** are very poisonous as is its **vapour**.

metal Any chemical **element** such as **iron** or **copper** that is reactive, has a crystalline structure, is shiny and has high **melting** and **boiling points**.

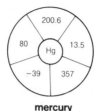

mercury

Metals produce **cations**, react with **acids**, are strong and hard, are **malleable** and **ductile**, are good conductors of heat and electricity and react with non-metals. 17% of elements are metals.

Pure metals are rarely used today. Most metals are used in the form of **alloys**. These play a vital part in our lives.

metalloid **Elements** that are neither **metals** nor **non-metals**. They are sometimes referred to as *semimetals*.

The best examples are germanium and **arsenic**. Such substances tend to have the physical properties of metals, in that they have a shiny appearance and a high **melting** and **boiling point** but the chemical properties of non-metals, e.g. do not react with **acids**. They are useful as **semiconductors**.

metamorphic rocks Rocks which have been formed from **igneous** or **sedimentary** rocks by high **temperatures** and/or **pressures**. Examples are **marble** and slate. See **rock cycle**.

methanal A toxic **gas** belonging to the family of **organic** compounds called *aldehydes*. Methanal is produced by the **oxidation** of **methanol**. It is an important chemical in the production of **thermosetting polymers**. See **urea/methanal resins**, **phenol**/methanal resins and **melamine**.

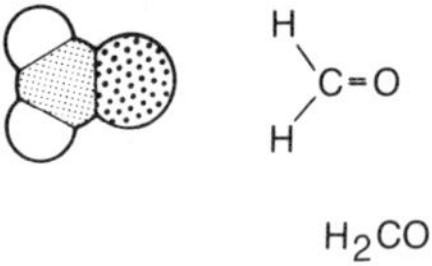

$$H_2CO$$

methanal

methane A gaseous **alkane**. It is the main constituent of **natural gas**. It is also released from **petroleum** whilst it is being processed. It burns readily to give **carbon dioxide** and **water** and is an industrial source of **hydrogen**.

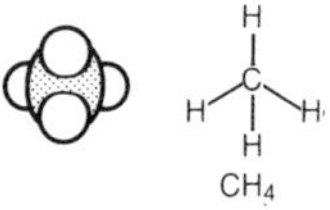

$$CH_4$$

methane

methanol An **alcohol**. It is a colourless **poisonous liquid**. Methanol is produced in large quantities from **synthesis gas** at high **temperature** and **pressure**:

$$CO(g) + 2H_2(g) \rightarrow CH_3OH(g)$$

$$CO_2(g) + 3H_2(g) \rightarrow CH_3OH(g) + H_2O(g)$$

Methanol is used in several ways:
(a) As a solvent;
(b) To produce **ethanoic acid**;
(c) To produce **methanal** and **thermosetting polymers**;
(d) As an **additive** to **unleaded petrol**;
(e) In the production of **methylated spirit**.

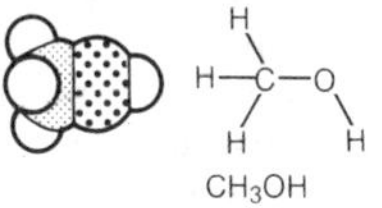

CH_3OH

methanol

methylated spirits A **mixture** of **ethanol** (90%), **methanol** (9.5%), pyridine (0.5%) and traces of a purple **dye**. This mixing is done to make the **ethanol** unfit for drinking. There is no excise tax on the mixture and so it is inexpensive. It is used as a **fuel** and a **solvent**.

methylbenzene (formerly **toluene**) This is an

aromatic hydrocarbon which is produced from
petroleum. It is used to make the explosive TNT
(TriNitro Toluene) and is a useful **solvent**.

methylbenzene

methyl orange   An **acid-base indicator**.

acid solution	alkaline solution
orange/red	yellow

methyl tertiary butyl ether (MTBE)   See
unleaded petrol.

mineral   1. The **inorganic** chemicals needed in
the human diet. Examples would be **iron**, **calcium** and **potassium**.
2. A naturally occurring inorganic chemical
which is used as a **raw material** in the chemical
industry. The major minerals used in the UK are
shown in the table opposite. See **ore**.

mineral extraction   Method of taking minerals
and **ores** from the ground. The main methods
are:
(a) Open-cast mining, for **limestone, clay, coal,
   phosphate, iron** ore.
(b) Underground mining and solution mining for
   coal, tin, gold, uranium, rock salt.

Mineral	Use
Clay	Building materials
Fluospar	**Plastics**
Gypsum	**Cement**
Limestone	Cement, **glass, paper, rubber**, building materials
Phosphates	**Fertilizers, detergents**
Potash	Potassium chemicals, **fertilizers**
Rock salt	**Detergents, soaps**, food, textiles, paper, **plastics, bleaches**
Sand	Building materials, **cement, glass, catalysts**
Sulphur	**Explosives, paints, plastics, dyes**, fertilizers

mineral Major mineral usage in the UK.

mineral processing The techniques of changing **minerals** and metallic **ores** into more useful forms. They are processed in standard ways. For example:
(a) Extraction;
(b) Crushing and grinding to a powder;
(c) Sorting according to size and properties;
(d) Removal of impurities;
(e) Chemical purification.

miscible Capable of being mixed. **Liquids** which can mix together completely are described as miscible. They can **dissolve** in each other, e.g. **water** and **ethanol**. They require **fractional distillation** to separate them. See **immiscible**.

mixture Two or more substances present in the same container. Examples are: **baking powder**, **air**, gunpowder, **petrol**, **methylated spirits**. Mixtures have several properties.
(a) Mixtures can be made in all proportions.
(b) Making mixtures does not involve the release or absorption of heat.
(c) The properties of a mixture are the properties of *all* the components.
(d) Mixtures can be separated by physical means.

ml Abbreviation for millilitre. 1000 ml = 1 **litre**.

mmHg Symbol representing the **unit** *millimetres of mercury*. It is a unit of **pressure**. One **atmosphere** pressure equals 760 mmHg. This is the **air** pressure which would support a column of **mercury** 760 mm high.

Mohs scale A scale used to express the hardness of solids by comparing them against ten standards. The hardness of **minerals** varies widely and so a scale such as this can be useful in helping to identify unknown specimens. On the scale, hardness increases from 1 to 10.

The unknown mineral can be tested against the standard ones; if the sample mineral scratches apatite but not feldspar, it will have a hardness of between 5 and 6. A fingernail will scratch a mineral with hardness 1 or 2, a 10p coin

Hardness	Standard mineral
1	**Talc**
2	**Rock salt** or **gypsum**
3	Calcite
4	Fluospar
5	Apatite (or window glass)
6	Feldspar
7	Quartz or flint
8	Topaz
9	Corundum
10	**Diamond**

Mohs scale

up to a hardness of 3, and a pocket penknife will scratch up to hardness 5.

Named after the German mineralogist Friedrich Mohs, 1773–1839.

molarity (M) The **concentration** of a **solution** expressed in **moles** per cubic decimetre of solution (**mol/dm³**). A solution containing 2 moles per dm³ is expressed as 2 M. See **molar solution**.

molar solution Where the **concentration** of solute is *one* **mole** per cubic decimetre of **solution** 1 mol/dm³. In other words, a solution where one mole of solute has been dissolved in the **solvent** and then sufficient solvent has been added to make 1000 cm³ of solution.

mol/dm³ A **unit** of **concentration**. 1 mol/dm³

means that one **mole** of substance would be present in one cubic decimetre (**dm³**) of the **solution**. The unit is sometimes written mol dm⁻³ and often given the symbol M, e.g. 2 M. See **molarity**.

mole The amount of a substance (**element** or **compound**) which contains **L** particles (L is the **Avogadro constant**).

L is defined as the number of **atoms** there are in 12 g of the **carbon**-12 **isotope**. It follows that the **mass** of one mole of an element or compound is the **relative atomic mass** (expressed in grammes). For example, one mole of

Oxygen	(O_2)	is $16 + 16$	$= 32$ g
Water	(H_2O)	is $2(1) + 16$	$= 18$ g
Ammonia	(NH_3)	is $14 + 3(1)$	$= 17$ g
Ethene	(C_2H_4)	is $2(12) + 4(1)$	$= 28$ g

molecule The smallest particle of an **element** or **compound** which exists independently. It contains **atoms** bonded together in a fixed whole number ratio:

Oxygen O_2	Phosphorus P_4
Nitrogen N_2	Carbon dioxide CO_2
Neon Ne	Water H_2O
Sulphur S_8	Hydrogen chloride HCl
Hydrogen H_2	

All organic compounds except **polymers** are molecules.

molecular formula Shows the number and types of **atoms** in the **molecule**. It tells us nothing about how the atoms are arranged, e.g. $C_4H_{10}O$ is the molecular formula of butanol and **ether** (ethoxyethane). See **empirical formula**, **structural formula**.

monatomic molecule A **molecule** which only contains one **atom**. Only the **noble gases** are monatomic. Because of their **electronic configurations** it is difficult for **noble** gas atoms to form **bonds**, and so they exist in the monatomic form.

monobasic acid An **acid** which contains only one **hydrogen atom** per **molecule** which can be replaced by a **metal**. Only normal salts can be formed — no **acid salts**. Examples include hydrochloric acid (HCl) and nitric acid (HNO_3).

monomer Any **compound** from which **polymers** are made, e.g. **ethene** $CH_2{=}CH_2$ forms **poly(ethene)** $(CH_2{-}CH_2)_n$.

monosaccharide The simplest kind of **sugar**. In these **compounds** there is a single **molecule** as opposed to two (or more) which have reacted together to form **disaccharides** or **polysaccharides**. Examples are glucose ($C_6H_{12}O_6$), fructose ($C_6H_{12}O_6$), and ribose ($C_5H_{10}O_5$).

mortar A **mixture** of **water**, **sand** and **cement** which is used to **bond** building materials.

multiple bonds **Bonds** which contain four or six **electrons**, two or three shared pairs are multiple bonds. **Double bonds** contain four electrons. **Triple bonds** contain six. Examples of **compounds** which contain multiple bonds are:

> **Ethene** C_2H_4 — double bond
> **Ethyne** C_2H_2 — triple bond

See **single bonds**.

nanometre A **unit** of length. It is 10^{-9} of a metre, that is 1 000 000 000 make 1 m. It is useful in measuring the length of **bonds**, e.g. $H-H$ bond length $= 0.074$ nm.

naphtha A **mixture** of **hydrocarbons** which is produced by the **fractional distillation** of **petroleum**. The **boiling points** of the **compounds** in the **mixture** are in the range 80–160 °C. Naphtha is usually subjected to **cracking**. **Ethene** is an important product of this process. Naphtha can be oxidized to give **ethanoic acid**.

native Describes an **element** which is found in nature uncombined with any other element.

natural fibres **Fibres** which are produced from either animal or plant sources. Examples are

cotton, flax, hemp, jute, **silk** and **wool**. See **synthetic**.

natural gas A **mixture** of mainly **hydro-carbon gases** which is found in deposits beneath the earth's surface. **Natural gas** and **petroleum** are often found together. **Methane** is usually the major constituent. The **inert** gas, **helium**, is sometimes present in the mixture. Natural gas is used as a **fuel** in both industry and the home.

neon A **noble gas** which is found in the **atmosphere** to a small extent. It forms no known **compounds** but is used to fill fluorescent tubes. A red glow is produced. Neon lights are often used for advertising signs.

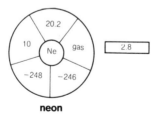

neon

neutral 1. A neutral **solution** is one which is neither acidic nor **alkaline**. Neutral solutions contains the same concentration of **hydroxide**

and **oxonium ions**. The **pH** of a neutral solution is seven at 25 °C.

2. A neutral **oxide** does not react with either **acids** or **alkalis**. The best example is **water**.

3. A neutral particle is one which does not have an electric charge, e.g. a **neutron**.

neutralization The process in which either the **pH** of an acidic **solution** is increased to 7 or the pH of an **alkaline** solution is decreased to 7. The resulting solution contains the same concentration of **oxonium** and **hydroxide ions**, that is, it is **neutral**.

An **acid** can be neutralized by the addition of a base or a **compound** such as a carbonate.

$HCl(aq) + NaOH(aq) \rightarrow NaCl(aq) + H_2O(l)$

$2HCl(aq) + CaCO_3(s) \rightarrow$
$CaCl_2(aq) + CO_2(g) + H_2O(l)$

Acid-base indicators show when neutralization is complete.

neutron One of the particles found in the **nucleus** of all **atoms** except **hydrogen**. It has approximately the same **mass** as the **proton** but no charge. See **nuclear reactions**.

nickel A **transition metal**. It is a magnetic substance which occurs as the **sulphide** and is oxidized to the **oxide**, reduced by **hydrogen** and then purified by using **carbon monoxide** gas:

$$Ni(s) + 4CO(g) \rightarrow Ni(CO)_4(g)$$

This reaction can be reversed at high **temperatures**, producing **pure** nickel.

Nickel can have a **valency** of 2, 3 or 4, but only nickel(II) **salts** are common. Nickel is used as a **catalyst**, in **alloys** (nichrome, coinage metal, stainless steel) and in plating.

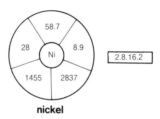

nickel

nitrate Salt of **nitric acid**, containing the $-NO_3$ group and with a **valency** of 1. A nitrate can be made by treating a metal **carbonate** or **oxide** with the dilute **acid**:

$$CuCO_3(s) + 2HNO_3(aq) \rightarrow$$
$$Cu(NO_3)_2(aq) + CO_2(g) + H_2O(l)$$

$$ZnO(s) + 2HNO_3(aq) \rightarrow$$
$$Zn(NO_3)_2(aq) + H_2O(l)$$

Nitrates are easily decomposed by heat. There are three kinds of reaction:

(a) $2KNO_3(s) \rightarrow 2KNO_2(s) + O_2(g)$

examples: sodium, potassium.

(b) $2Cu(NO_3)_2(s) \rightarrow 2CuO(s) + O_2(g) + 4NO_2(g)$

all metal nitrates other than shown in (a) and (c).

(c) $2AgNO_3(s) \rightarrow 2Ag(s) + 2NO_2(g) + O_2(g)$

examples: silver, mercury.

Nitrates are important **fertilizers**, e.g. **sodium nitrate** and **ammonium nitrate**. If used incorrectly they can lead to serious water **pollution**.

nitric acid (HNO$_3$) A colourless, corrosive **liquid** made from **ammonia** by **oxidation** over a **platinum**/rhodium **catalyst**. There are three stages:

$$4NH_3(g) + 5O_2(g) \rightarrow 4NO(g) + 6H_2O(g)$$

$$4NO(g) + 2O_2(g) \rightarrow 4NO_2(g)$$

$$4NO_2(g) + 2H_2O(l) + O_2(g) \rightarrow 4HNO_3(aq)$$

The acid is distilled to a **concentration** of 68% and can be prepared in the laboratory by heating a **nitrate** with **concentrated sulphuric acid**:

$$KNO_3(s) + H_2SO_4(l) \rightarrow KHSO_4(s) + HNO_3(g)$$

Nitric acid is a vigorous **oxidizing agent** used in the production of **fertilizers**, **explosives**, **dyes** and the **polymer**, **nylon**. The **salts** of nitric acid are termed nitrates. See **nitrogen oxides**, **nitrites**.

nitrites Salts of nitrous acid (HNO_2). The **sodium** and **potassium** salts can be made by heating the nitrate:

$$2NaNO_3(s) \rightarrow 2NaNO_2(s) + O_2(g)$$

They are used in the **curing** of meats.

nitrogen (N₂) A non-metallic **element** in group v of the periodic table. It is an unreactive, **diatomic** gas which forms about 78% of the **atmosphere**. It is produced by the **fractional distillation** of liquid **air**.

Nitrogen is an important chemical because of the need for **nitric acid** and **ammonia**. It is *fixed* from the atmosphere in the **Haber process**.

Nitrogen gas is used to provide an **inert** atmosphere, for example, in:

(a) **Annealing steel**;
(b) **Silicon** chip production;
(c) Food packaging;
(d) **Glass** production.

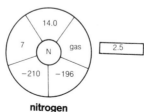

nitrogen

Liquid nitrogen is used in the refrigeration of such items as medical samples and the transportation of food.

See **nitrogen oxides, nitrogen cycle**.

nitrogen cycle The process which shows the ways in which annimals, plants and humans are involved in the chemical links between **nitrogen, ammonia** and **nitrates**. Nitrogen is fixed from the **atmosphere** by:

(a) The **Haber process**;
(b) Electrical discharges (lightning);
(c) Action by soil bacteria.

The nitrates in the soil are taken up by plants which are then eaten by animals. Both animal and plant **protein** can rot and revert to ammonia. Animals also excrete urine which decomposes to ammonia.

Nitrogen is returned to the atmosphere by the action of other bacteria.

Despite human extraction of **nitrogen** from the air in the Haber process the amount of nitrogen in the atmosphere remains approximately constant.

nitrogen oxides

Nitrogen monoxide NO	A colourless **gas** which can be produced by the action of *moderately* **concentrated nitric acid** on **copper**. The gas reacts *immediately* with

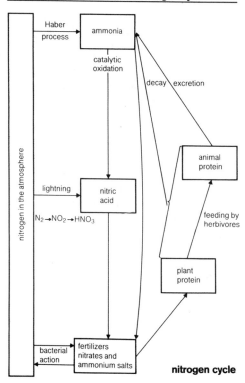

nitrogen cycle

	oxygen to form nitrogen dioxide: $2NO(g) + O_2(g) \rightarrow 2NO_2(g)$
Nitrogen dioxide NO_2	A brown gas. It has a choking smell and irritates the lungs and windpipe. Breathing it can lead to death from pneumonia. It can be produced in the laboratory by the action of concentrated **nitric acid** on **copper**.
Nitrous oxide N_2O	A colourless gas with a sweetish smell. It is an anaesthetic and is used in dentistry. It is sometimes called laughing gas.

See **greenhouse gases** and **acidification**.

noble gases (or **inert gases**) Elements in **group** 0 of the **periodic table**. They are all very unreactive **monatomic** gases which occur in the **atmosphere** to small extents.

Their **electronic configurations** lead to very stable chemistry and the elements show no tendency to lose or gain **electrons**. Because of this, they find it hard to form **compounds**. Compounds do exist of the more massive elements, e.g. XeF_4, but these are rare.

All the gases are produced commercially by the **fractional distillation** of liquid air, except **helium** which is recovered from **natural gas**. See **neon, argon, krypton, xenon**.

noble gas structure Stable, unreactive ele-

ments. Noble gases have eight **electrons** in their *outer* **shell**. This is a stable **electronic configuration** because the eight electrons completely fill a part of the shell making it difficult to add another or take one away. When elements form **ions**, the ions which are formed have the noble gas configuration, as the table shows.

| Element | Ion | Electronic configuration | | Noble gas |
		atom	ion	
Sodium	Na^+	2·8·1	2·8	Neon
Fluorine	F^-	2·7	2·8	Neon
Calcium	Ca^{2+}	2·8·8·2	2·8·8	Argon
Sulphur	S^{2-}	2·8·6	2·8·8	Argon
Aluminium	Al^{3+}	2·8·3	2·8	Neon
Bromine	Br^-	2·8·18·7	2·8·18·8	Krypton

non-metals Elements which have either molecular structures, and thus are **gases** at **room temperature**, or are **solids** or **liquids** with low **melting** and **boiling points**; or **giant structures** with **covalent** bonding. Typical properties of non-metals are as follows:
(a) They have poor **conductivity**.
(b) They do not react with **acids**.
(c) They produce **acidic oxides**.
(d) They form **covalent** compounds.
(e) They give rise to **anions**.
Examples include: the **halogens**, the **noble gases**, oxygen, sulphur, carbon, nitrogen.

nuclear reactions Reactions in which new **compounds** are not formed but changes occur in the nuclei and new **elements** can be formed. They are very different from normal chemical reactions. Most elements have stable and unstable isotopes, e.g.

carbon-12	carbon-13	carbon-14
stable		unstable

But some have no stable **isotopes**, e.g. **uranium, plutonium**. Whether an isotope is unstable depends on the numbers of **neutrons** and **protons** in the **nucleus**. When an isotope is unstable, several reactions can occur:

(a) The isotope can split — fission can occur. This creates two stable isotopes. Neutrons are also released and lots of energy is released.

(b) A neutron can decay into a proton and an electron:

$$_0^1n \rightarrow {}_1^1p + {}_{-1}^0e$$

The electron is expelled from the nucleus (**beta particle**) and the atomic number of the atom increases by 1, e.g.:

$$_{82}^{209}Pb \rightarrow {}_{83}^{209}Bi + {}_{-1}^0e$$

This creates a new element. There is no change in mass.

(c) An alpha particle is expelled from the atom:

$$^{238}_{92}U \rightarrow\ ^{234}_{90}Th + ^{4}_{2}He$$

(d) An unstable atom can emit **gamma rays**. This often occurs after the emission of a beta particle. See **half-life**.

These nuclear reactions have been used by us in many ways. Nuclear power stations use the heat produced in the **fission** of uranium, plutonium or thorium isotopes. The heat turns water into steam which drives a turbine producing electricity. This same source of energy is also used by some countries in the form of bombs. These have terrible destructive powers.

Isotopes producing **gamma rays** are used to destroy bacteria in food processing and *cancerous* cells in the body. Isotopes are also used in industry for a variety of analytical purposes, e.g. detecting cracks in pipelines.

Scientists are striving to produce useful energy from **fusion** reactions and if this is possible it will provide a source of **electricity** which is not dependent upon **coal** or **petroleum**.

The products of radioactive decay (**radioactivity**) are dangerous as they can produce harmful effects on the body including leukaemia and cancers. Great care has to be taken when using radioactive materials.

nucleons Particles found in the **nucleus** of the **atom**, that is, **protons** and **neutrons**.

nucleus The part of an **atom** where the **mass** is concentrated. It contains **protons** and **neutrons** and is usually pictured as being the compact centre of a spherical atom.

Electrons move around the nucleus. The nucleus has a positive charge and in the neutral atom this is balanced by the charges on the electrons.

The hydrogen-1 **isotope** is the only atom whose nuclei contain no neutrons. See diagram. See also **nuclear reactions**.

a nucleus of
carbon – 12 contains
6 protons and 6
neutrons

a nucleus of
carbon – 14 contains
6 protons and 8
neutrons

nucleus Different isotopes showing different nuclei.

nylon A family of **polyamide polymers**. The most common of them is *Nylon 6.6*. This synthetic **fibre** has great strength. Its uses include fabrics (shirts, cloth), yarns (stocking, knitwear), carpets, ropes and nets.   Nylon is useful because it will not rot, it does not absorb **water** but it does stretch. This is useful in ropes and stockings. It is often mixed with other fibres, e.g. wool, to get the correct balance of properties.

nylon The most common nylon, nylon 6.6.

octane A **hydrocarbon** with the **formula** C_8H_{18}. See **alkanes, octane number**.

octane rating (or **octane number)** A measure of the **anti-knock** qualities of **petrol**. **Petrol** and **air mixtures** have to explode at exactly the correct moment in an internal combustion engine. If the wrong kind of **fuel** is used ignition of the **mixture** can occur *before* it should. This leads to the characteristic sound of *pinking* (or *knocking*).

The higher the rating, the better the fuel is. Four star petrol has an octane rating of 98. The greater the proportion of *branched* **hydrocarbon** molecules in the fuel, the greater the rating will be.

Octane ratings can be raised by adding substances such as tetraethyl lead. This unfortunately leads to lead **pollution** in the **atmosphere**. See **unleaded petrol**.

oil A **liquid fat** e.g. melted butter, olive oil,

sunflower oil, etc. The word is sometimes used in place of **petroleum**.

olefin See **alkenes**.

oleum A **solution** of **sulphur(VI) oxide** in **concentrated sulphuric acid**. It is a very corrosive substance and is a vigorous **oxidizing agent**. See **contact process**.

ore A naturally occurring substance from which an **element** can be extracted. Examples are shown below. See **mineral**.

Element	Ore
Aluminium	**Bauxite**
Chlorine	**Rock salt**
Copper	Chalcopyrite ($CuFeS_2$)
	Bornite (Cu_5FeS_4)
Iron	Haematite (Fe_2O_3)
	Magnetite (Fe_3O_4)
Lead	Galena (PbS)
Zinc	Zinc blende (ZnS)

ores Elements and the ores extracted from them.

organic Material that is organic is produced by or found in plants or animals.

organic chemistry The study of **compounds** of **carbon**. It does not include carbonates, **carbon**

dioxide, etc. See **inorganic chemistry**.

oxidation A process which causes a chemical change by reacting with oxygen. A substance undergoes oxidation if it:

(a) Gains oxygen: $2Mg(s) + O_2(g) \rightarrow 2MgO(s)$
(b) Loses hydrogen: $CH_4(g) + Cl_2(g) \rightarrow$
$CH_3Cl(l) + HCl(g)$
(c) Loses electrons: $Cu(s) \rightarrow Cu^{2+}(aq) + 2e^-$

See **oxidizing agent, reduction, redox**.

oxide A compound formed between an **element** and **oxygen** only. Oxides can be formed by:
(a) Direct combustion of the elements;
(b) Oxidizing compounds;
(c) The action of heat on a **carbonate**, a **hydroxide** or some **nitrates**.
Examples of oxides are

$$2Mg(s) + O_2(g) \rightarrow 2MgO(s)$$

$$CH_4(g) + 2O_2(g) \rightarrow CO_2(g) + 2H_2O(g)$$

$$CuCO_3(s) \rightarrow CuO(s) + CO_2(g)$$

$$Pb(OH)_2(s) \rightarrow PbO(s) + H_2O(g)$$

$$2Zn(NO_3)_2(s) \rightarrow 2ZnO(s) + 4NO_2(g) + O_2(g)$$

Oxides can be reduced to the element with a suitable **reducing agent**, e.g. **hydrogen, carbon** or carbon monoxide. See **basic oxide, acidic oxide, amphoteric oxide**.

oxidizing agent A substance which causes the **oxidation** of another substance. When this happens the oxidizing agent is reduced.

Common oxidizing agents are:

Oxygen	O_2
Chlorine	Cl_2
Ozone	O_3
Hydrogen peroxide	H_2O_2
Potassium manganate(VII)	$KMnO_4$

Examples of oxidizing agents at work include:

$$Mg(s) + O_2(g) \rightarrow 2MgO(s)$$

$$Cl_2(g) + 2Na(s) \rightarrow 2NaCl(s)$$

$$H_2O_2(aq) + H_2S(g) \rightarrow 2H_2O(l) + S(s)$$

oxonium ion (H_3O^+) Formed by the loss of an **electron** from a **hydrogen atom**. It leads to the formation of a hydrogen **ion**. This is a **proton**.

The proton is such a small, reactive particle that in **aqueous solution** it forms **bonds** to **water molecules**. More than one water molecule is probably involved but, for simplicity only one is usually shown.

$$H \rightarrow H^+ + e^-$$

$$H^+ \cdots O \qquad H_3O^+(aq)$$

It can be used in ionic equations in place of $H^+(aq)$:

$$H_3O^+(aq) + OH^-(aq) \rightarrow 2H_2O(l)$$

$$\text{acid} \quad + \quad \text{alkali}$$

oxygen (O_2) A gaseous, non-metallic **element** in **group** VI of the **periodic table**. It makes up 21% of the **atmosphere**. It is a vigorous **oxidizing agent** and is vital for the **respiration** of plants and animals.

It is a reactive gas, readily forming **oxides** with most **elements**. It is obtained industrially by the **fractional distillation** of liquefied air and in the laboratory by the decomposition of **hydrogen peroxide**:

$$2H_2O_2(aq) \rightarrow 2H_2O(l) + O_2(g)$$

A **catalyst** such as manganese(IV) oxide is usually used.

Oxygen is a colourless, odourless **diatomic** gas. It is **neutral** and is only slightly soluble in water (40 cm^3 per cubic decimetre). It is sufficiently soluble to allow fish and other aquatic life to live in water. Problems arise if the oxygen in water drops to too low a level. Then, fish suffocate and die. Such a drop in the **concentration** of oxygen is usually caused by **pollution**. See **eutrophic**.

The chemical test for oxygen is to plunge a glowing splint into the gas. If the gas is oxygen, the splint will relight. The gas will also make anything which is already burning in air, burn much more fiercely.

Oxygen is used extensively in steel-making and welding, as a rocket propellant together with kerosene or hydrogen, and for life-support systems in medicine or breathing apparatus. It is also used to produce other chemicals.

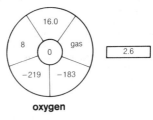

oxygen

ozone (O_3) An **allotrope** of **oxygen** where the molecule is *tri*atomic $O_3(g)$. It is a blue gas and is a very powerful **oxidizing agent** and extremely poisonous. It can be formed from oxygen by passing a spark through the **gas**:

$$3O_2(g) \rightarrow 2O_3(g)$$

Ozone is a powerful germicide, and its great oxidizing power makes it useful, in very high dilution, for ventilating spaces where fresh air has limited access e.g. underground railways. It is also used in bleaching textiles, **paper** and **oil**, and in purifying the water in swimming pools. Ozone is found in the stratosphere. See **ozone layer**, **Earth's atmosphere**.

ozone layer Part of the **Earth's atmosphere** which contains **ozone**. About one molecule in every 10 000 000 in the Earth's atmosphere is ozone. Although this doesn't sound a lot, because the atmosphere is so large, there are billions of tonnes of the gas which is concentrated in a 20 km thick region round the Earth in the stratosphere. Here it provides protection against **ultraviolet (u.v.) radiation** from the sun. The ozone molecules stop most of the u.v. reaching the Earth where it would cause great damage to crops and marine life and to human skin.

The u.v. breaks down the ozone into oxygen, but ozone is continuously reformed by the action of u.v. radiation on oxygen. Every day, on average, 300 million tonnes of ozone are destroyed and produced in the stratosphere.

Since 1980, the amount of ozone in the stratosphere has been reduced, particularly over the poles where the coverage can become thin during the spring. This reduction is blamed on atmospheric **pollutants** such as **CFCs**. See **greenhouse effect**, **greenhouse gases**, **pollution**.

paint A chemical **mixture** which is used to protect and decorate materials. All paints contain:
(a) **Pigments** to provide colour;

(b) Binders to dissolve the other materials;
(c) Thinners to make the paint easy to apply.
   Other **additives** might include:
(d) Drying agents to speed up the drying process;
(e) Silicones to give resistance against the weather;
(f) **Biocides** to protect against fungal attack;
(g) Extenders to provide bulk to the paint.

paper Cellulose fibres which have been hydrated and formed into a mat. Paper which is used for writing on is usually treated (*sized*) in order to make it less **porous**, and bleached in order to make it lighter in colour. Now much paper which is used is **recycled**.

paraffin Fuel obtained from **petroleum**. It has a boiling range of 160–250 °C.
   Paraffin wax consists of a mixture of solid **hydrocarbons**. It is used to make candles. See **kerosine**.

pascal The SI unit of **pressure**. One **atmosphere** pressure is about 100 kilopascals (100 kPa). One pascal is equivalent to a force of 1 Newton on 1 square metre ($1 \, \text{Nm}^{-2}$).

passive Describes a **metal** which possesses a surface layer of **oxide** which makes it unreactive. **Aluminium** has such a layer and **iron** can be given one by dipping the metal into **concentrated nitric acid**.

pasteurization A heat-treatment process to reduce the number of micro-organisms present in food in order to extend its shelf-life. Milk is pasteurized by being heated to 71.7 °C for at least 15 seconds. Pasteurized milk will keep in the fridge for 4–5 days. See **UHT, sterilization**.

pectin A **carbohydrate polymer** which is found in many soft fruits. Pectin is useful in the formation of **gels** and is necessary in getting jams to set.

peptide A **compound** formed when two or more **amino acids** react together. If three or more amino acids are involved the term **polypeptide** is usually used. **Proteins** consist of long polypeptide chains which are often linked together in a variety of ways.   Peptides contain the *peptide link*:

percentage composition What proportion of a **compound** is made up of any given **element**.

This is usually expressed in percentage terms.

Element	% by mass of: carbon	hydrogen
Methane CH_4	75	25
Ethyne C_2H_2	92	8

percentage composition

Knowing the percentage composition of a compound it is possible to work out its **empirical formula**. For example:

A compound is known to have a percentage composition of: Ca 40% C 12% O 48%.

To find the *molar* ratio of the elements in the compound, divide each figure by the respective A_r value (Ca) $^{40}/_{40}=1$ (C) $^{12}/_{12}=1$ (O) $^{48}/_{16}=3$.

The molar ratio is 1:1:3.

Therefore the ratio of the atoms is: 1:1:3.

The empirical formula is: $CaCO_3$.

period In the **periodic table**, the horizontal rows of **elements**. There are seven in all. See **group**.

periodic table A way of presenting all the **ele-**

ments so as to show their similarities and differences (see overleaf).

The elements are arranged in increasing order of **atomic number (Z)** as you go from left to right across the table. For example:

Period 3							
Na	Mg	Al	Si	P	S	Cl	Ar
11	12	13	14	15	16	17	18

The horizontal rows are called **periods** and the vertical rows, **groups**. A **noble gas** is found at the right hand side of each period.

Period	1	He
	2	Ne
	3	Ar
	4	Kr
	5	Xe
	6	Rn

There is a progression from **metals** to **nonmetals** across each period.

Similar elements are found in a group, e.g. these elements have a similar **electronic configuration** and are found in the same group, e.g.:

group I	alkali metals	Li	Na	K
group VII	halogens	F	Cl	Br	I

The number of **electrons** in the outer shell is the

Group																		
I	II	III	IV	V	VI	VII	0

periodic table

Symbol — H
Atomic number — 1

transition elements

Group I	II											III	IV	V	VI	VII	0
																	He 2
Li 3	Be 4											B 5	C 6	N 7	O 8	F 9	Ne 10
Na 11	Mg 12											Al 13	Si 14	P 15	S 16	Cl 17	Ar 18
K 19	Ca 20	Sc 21	Ti 22	V 23	Cr 24	Mn 25	Fe 26	Co 27	Ni 28	Cu 29	Zn 30	Ga 31	Ge 32	As 33	Se 34	Br 35	Kr 36
Rb 37	Sr 38	Y 39	Zr 40	Ni 41	Mo 42	Tc 43	Ru 44	Rh 45	Pd 46	Ag 47	Cd 48	In 49	Sn 50	Sb 51	Te 52	I 53	Xe 54
Cs 55	Ba 56	La 57	Hf 72	Ta 73	W 74	Re 75	Os 76	Ir 77	Pt 78	Au 79	Hg 80	Tl 81	Pb 82	Bi 83	Po 84	At 85	Rn 86
Fr 87	Ra 88	Ac 89	Unq 104	Unp 105													

Ce 58	Pr 59	Nd 60	Pm 61	Sm 62	Eu 63	Gd 64	Tb 65	Dy 66	Ho 67	Er 68	Tm 69	Yb 70	Lu 71
Th 90	Pa 91	U 92	Np 93	Pu 94	Am 95	Cm 96	Bk 97	Cf 98	Es 99	Fm 100	Md 101	No 102	Lr 103

same as the number of the group, e.g. group I:

lithium	2·1
sodium	2·8·1
potassium	2·8·8·1

The block of elements between groups II and III are called the **transition metals**. These are similar in many ways: they produce coloured compounds, have variable **valency** and are often used as **catalysts**. Elements 58 to 71 are known as *lanthanide* or rare earth elements. These elements are found on earth in only very small amounts.

Elements 90 to 103 are known as the *actinide* elements. They include most of the well known elements which are found in **nuclear reactions**. The elements with larger atomic numbers than 92 do not occur naturally. They have all been produced artificially by bombarding other elements with particles. **Plutonium** is formed in nuclear reactors.

Elements with atomic numbers of 104 and above are not being named after famous scientists or places. They are now being named in a systematic way according to their atomic number. For example:

element 104 is *Unnilquadium*

un	=1	Symbol
nil	=0	*Unq*
quad	=4	

element 118 would be *Ununoc*tium	un	=1	Symbol
	un	=1	*Uuo*
	oct	=8	

permanent hardness   See **hardness of water**.

peroxide   A **compound** containing the O_2^{2-} **ion** or $-O_2$ **group**. The best example is **hydrogen peroxide** (H_2O_2). The peroxides of **alkali** metals are also known. Hydrogen peroxide can be made by the action of **acid** on these:

$$Na_2O_2(s) + 2HCl(aq) \rightarrow 2NaCl(aq) + H_2O_2(aq)$$

Peroxides are vigorous **oxidizing agents**. Hydrogen peroxide can be used in dilute **solution** as a **disinfectant** and a **bleach**.

perspex   Trade name for the **polymer, poly(methylmethacrylate)**.

pesticide   See **biocide**.

petrochemical   A chemical which has been made from **petroleum**. Examples include **ethene** and **propene**. These chemicals are used in the manufacture of other chemicals, e.g. **poly(ethene)** and **poly(propene)**. Petrochemicals are *intermediates* in the production of finished products.

petrol   A mixture of **hydrocarbons** which is

used as a **fuel** in internal **combustion engines**. It is produced from **petroleum** in a refinery. It is principally a **mixture** of C_5—C_{10} **alkanes** obtained by both straight **fractional distillation** and by **cracking** and **reforming**. Petrol is also known as gasoline or motor spirit. See **octane rating, unleaded petrol**.

petroleum The **mixture** of **hydrocarbons** which are found in the Earth's crust, e.g. **natural gas** and crude **oil**. It has been produced over millions of years from the remains of marine animals and plant organisms. It is the **raw material** for the petrochemical industry and is the source of our **petrol, diesel** fuel, heating oil, **fuel** oil and **gas** supplies. Vast reserves of petroleum are found in the Middle East, the United States, the Soviet Union, Central America and the North Sea.

Petroleum has replaced **coal** as the chief source of raw materials for the chemical industry. But the supply of petroleum will not last forever and the search is now on for the substance which will replace it in our lives.

How petroleum is converted into useful products is described under **refining**. See also **fractional distillation**.

pH A scale for measuring the acidity or alkalinity of a **solution**.

acidity increasing	neutral	alkalinity increasing

0	3	7	10	14

The lower the value, the more acidic is the solution, i.e. the larger the **concentration** of **oxonium ions** there is within it. A **neutral** solution, where the concentrations of oxonium and hydroxide ions are equal, has a pH of 7 at 25 °C.

The pH of a solution is the negative logarithm (base 10) of the concentration of oxonium ions (mol/dm³). Thus,

$$pH = -\log_{10}[H_3O^+]$$

Example:
The pH of a solution whose concentration is 0.1 mol/**dm**³ is $-\log(0.1)=1$

Substance at a concentration of 1 mol/dm³	pH
Strong acid (HCl)	0
Weak acid (CH₃COOH)	4
Water	7
Ammonia solution	10
Strong alkali (NaOH)	14

pH   pHs of common substances.

phase change (or **change of state**) A change which occurs when a substance goes from one physical **state** to another

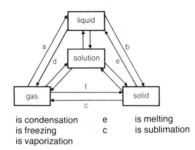

a	is condensation	e	is melting
b	is freezing	c	is sublimation
d	is vaporization		

phase change Possible phases in a chemical system.

phenol A colourless crystalline **aromatic solid**, which turns pink on exposure to **air** and light.

Phenol is made by reacting **benzene** with **propene** ($CH_3CH=CH_2$) and then oxidizing the product. It is a very corrosive chemical and is **poisonous**. 35% of phenol production is used in the production of *phenol/methanal* polymers and a further 27% in the production of the transparent *poly(carbonates)* materials and *epoxy resins*. It is also used to make *nylon, dyes* and detergents. Disinfectant and many household products are based on similar molecules to phenol, i.e. compounds with similar (or better) disinfectant properties but which are less corrosive, e.g. T.C.P. and Dettol.

The O—H group in phenol has an acidic **hydrogen** and **salts** can be formed:

$$C_6H_5O^- Na^+(s)$$

C_6H_5OH

phenol

phenol/methanal   resins Dark   coloured, **thermo-setting, condensation polymers** made from **phenol** and **methanal**. The polymers have been used for electrical fittings because of their good electrical insulating properties, and for such items as saucepan handles because of their poor conduction of heat. The first **plastic** materials to be made were produced from these resins but, for everyday items, their use has largely been replaced by similar materials which can be coloured. However, they are used for rocket nosecones and other heatshields. See **melamine, urea/methanal resins**.

phenolphthalein An **indicator** used to follow

acid-base reactions. The molecular structure of the **compound** is based on the **phenol** molecule.

acid solution	alkaline solution
←	→
colourless	red

phosphates Salts of **phosphoric**(v) **acid**. Phosphoric acid is a *tri*basic acid and, therefore, gives rise to three kinds of salts:

(a) Sodium phosphate Na_3PO_4
(b) Sodium hydrogenphosphate Na_2HPO_4
(c) Sodium dihydrogenphosphate NaH_2PO_4

Phosphates are used in **fertilizers** to replace the **phosphorus**-containing compounds in the soil. It comes in several forms.

Superphosphate is a mixture of calcium sulphate and calcium dihydrogenphosphate $(Ca(H_2PO_4)_2)$. A mixture of ammonium nitrate and ammonium hydrogenphosphate $(NH_4)_2HPO_4$ is made by reacting **ammonia** with a mixture of **phosphoric (v)** and **nitric acids**. Calcium phosphate is the chief constituent of animal bones and phosphates are used extensively in washing powders and **detergents**.

Slag from **blast furnaces** is put directly onto the soil since it contains calcium phosphate.

phosphoric(v) acid (H_3PO_4) A tribasic acid which gives rise to three kinds of **phosphate**. It is a **solid** at **room temperature** but is usually sold as a viscous **solution** in **water**. It is used for rust-proofing **steel** by forming a protective layer of iron phosphate. It is also used in the food and drug industries but most (90%) of the production goes to produce **fertilizers**. See **phosphates**.

phosphorus (P₄) A solid non-metallic **element** in **group** v of the **periodic table**. Three **allotropes** exist: white, red and black phosphorus. The information in the chart refers to *white* phosphorus.

The allotropes have very different physical properties, e.g. **crystal** structure, **density, melting** and **boiling points**.

White phosphorus is very **poisonous** and has to be kept under water because it bursts into **flame** when it comes into contact with air, forming the **oxide**:

$$P_4(s) + 5O_2(g) \rightarrow P_4O_{10}(s)$$

Rocks containing phosphorus compounds are quite common in the Earth's crust and phosphorus is an important element for the maintenance of life. Plants need it and so it is a necessary component of **fertilizers**, e.g. **superphosphate**. (See **phosphates**.) Some **enzymes** used in **respiration** also contain the element. Animal bones contain phosphates. In earlier days phosphorus was used extensively in making the heads of matches. It has since been banned.

Matches nowadays contain phosphorus sulphide, and indeed in 'safety matches' the phosphorus sulphide is located on the side of the box, hence the match will only strike on the box. Over 90% of phosphorus produced today goes to make **phosphoric(v) acid**.

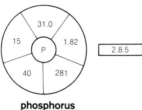

phosphorus

photochemical reactions Chemical reactions which are brought about by these. The process of photography depends on these. When silver bromide is exposed to light it decomposes:

$$2AgBr(s) \rightarrow 2Ag(s) + Br_2(g)$$

The black part of the negative of a film is a thin layer of **silver**. This is then processed to produce the final pictures.

Photosynthesis is the most important photochemical **reaction**. Our existence on this planet depends on it.

Other examples are the reaction between **hydrogen** and **chlorine** which can be started off by a bright light, e.g. burning magnesium:

$$H_2(g) + Cl_2(g) \rightarrow 2HCl(g)$$

In hot areas of the world, e.g. California, where there are a lot of vehicle exhaust fumes, photochemical *smog* can be produced by the reaction of the exhaust fumes. This is an acrid haze which is very unpleasant.

The **bleaching** action of the sun is also a photochemical reaction, as is the conversion of cholesterol in the skin into **vitamin** D.

In all these reactions light provides the **energy** that makes the reactions work.

photosynthesis A **photochemical** process in which **carbon dioxide** and **water** are converted into **carbohydrate** and **oxygen**:

$$6CO_2(g) + 6H_2O(l) \rightarrow C_6H_{12}O_2(s) + 6O_2(g)$$

This occurs in the leaves of plants and is the means whereby plants obtain their food. It also puts oxygen back into the **atmosphere**.

The reaction is catalysed by **chlorophyll** and sunlight provides the **energy** for the reaction.

physical change A change to a substance which involves changes in its physical **properties** with no alterations to chemical properties.

physical chemistry The study of the physical **properties** of **elements** and **compounds** and the relationship between their chemical properties and physical properties.

pickling 1. The treatment of **metals** with (usually warm dilute) **acid** in order to remove the surface layer of **oxide** so that they can be painted or treated in some way. It is necessary to pickle **steel** if it has been allowed to cool down in the **air**.
2. Treatment of foods with **vinegar** in order to preserve them for eating at a later date. Chutneys, sauces and pickles are examples.

pigment A chemical which gives colour to a material. Pigments may be **organic** and be produced from **petroleum** and natural sources, or **inorganic** and be based on **metal oxides**. The white pigment, titanium oxice (TiO_2) makes up 70% of all pigments used.

pitchblende An **oxide ore** of **uranium** which also contains radium and thorium.

planar A **molecule** which has all its **atoms** in the same plane. In other words, it is flat. All **linear** and triatomic molecules must be planar. Boron trifluoride is planar. Other planar molecules include:

H_2O	C_2H_2	CO	HCl
CO_2	SiO_2	NO_2	N_2

planar Boron trifluoride is planar.

Most **carbon** compounds are non-planar because of the **tetrahedral** arrangement of atoms around the carbon atom. Most alkenes are non-planar but **ethene** is an exception.

Propene is non-planar because the three hydrogen atoms attached to the carbon atom are above or below the other atoms.

ethene is planar   but propene is not

planar

plaster A material used to coat walls to produce a smooth surface which can be painted or papered. Plaster consists of a **mixture** of **lime** and **sand** which is mixed with **water** just before it is applied.

plaster of Paris A form of **gypsum** which has had half of the **water of crystallization** removed by heating. When **water** is added to plaster of Paris, a chemical reaction takes place to re-form gypsum.

$$CaSO_4.H_2O + H_2O \rightarrow CaSO_4.2H_2O$$

This is accompanied by a slight increase in **volume** which makes plaster of Paris ideal for making copies of artifacts in moulds.

plastic 1. Capable of being shaped or moulded by **heat** and **pressure**.
2. **Synthetic polymers**, e.g. **poly(ethene)**, **nylon**, etc. Over 30 different types of polymers exist and by combining them it is now possible to produce a synthetic substance with specific properties. See **thermosetting**, **thermoplastic**.

plasticizer An **additive** which makes **polymers** and other materials more **flexible** and better able to withstand being hit.

platinum A **transition metal** which is used as a **catalyst** in the chemical industry. It is also used as a metal for jewellery and as inert

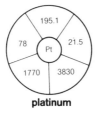

platinum

electrodes in **electrolysis**. It is expensive because it is useful and rare. Platinum occurs in nature as the **element**.

plutonium An artificial element. It is made in nuclear reactors from the 238 **isotope** of **uranium** by the absorption of a **neutron**:

$$^{238}_{92}U + ^{1}_{0}n \rightarrow ^{239}_{92}U \text{ (this is unstable)}$$

$$^{239}_{92}U \rightarrow ^{239}_{93}Np + ^{0}_{-1}e \textbf{ (beta particle)}$$

Neptunium−239 is also unstable:

$$^{239}_{93}Np \rightarrow ^{239}_{94}Pu + ^{0}_{-1}e \text{ (beta particle)}$$

Uranium−239 and neptunium−239 have **half-lives** of 20 minutes and two days respectively, and so soon decay. The **half-life** of plutonium−239 is over 24 000 years and so is fairly stable.

Plutonium is used in bombs and as a fuel for nuclear reactors, such as fast breeder reactors. The cores of these reactors are surrounded by uranium−238 which is converted to plutonium−239 (in the way shown above) while the reactor is working. In this way it is possible to produce more **fuel** than is used in the reactor.

Plutonium is a toxic and dangerous chemical and must be handled with great care. Great controversies surround its use.

plutonium

plywood A wooden **laminated** material. Plywood is made up of layers of wood or **veneer** glued together. The grain of adjacent layers runs at right angles to each other. Plywood is stronger than a similar **mass** of wood.

poison A substance which is harmful if taken into the body and which will lead to death or injury. Poisons can be breathed in, e.g. hydrogen cyanide (HCN), **carbon monoxide** (CO) or **lead** fumes in the air; they may be eaten or drunk, e.g. **arsenic**(III) oxide, strychnine, or paraquat; they may pass into the body through the skin, e.g. **benzene** and nerve gases.

Radiation from nuclear **isotopes** can also be viewed as a poison.

pollution Dangerous or dirty materials harmful to the environment or life. Pollution can occur when waste materials are not treated properly or when **toxic** materials escape from containers.

Examples are:

(a) Litter that is thrown away on the streets or in the countryside.

(b) Exhaust gases from engines and factories enter the air.

(c) **Fertilizers** from farms are allowed to enter streams and rivers.

(d) **Petroleum** escaping from tankers and being washed up onto a beach.

(e) **Toxic** chemicals are dumped in places from which they can escape into the ground water.
See **acid rain**, **global warming**.

poly-   Prefix used in the naming of chemicals to indicate that the **compound** is a **polymer**. See entries beginning **poly-**.

polyamides   Synthetic polymers which contain the *amide* group of **atoms**. Some **compounds** are usually known by the name **nylon**. Polyamides are **condensation** polymers.

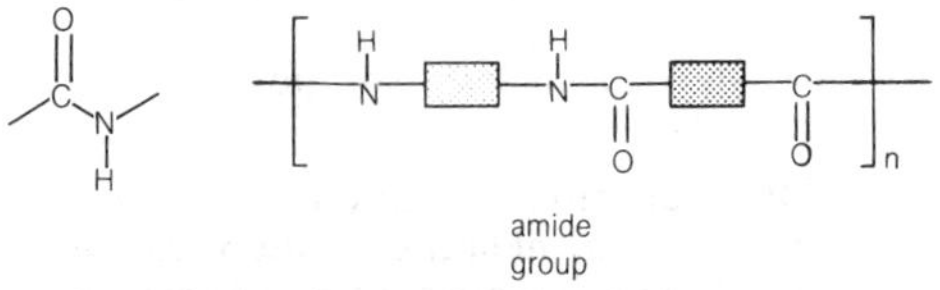

amide group

polyamides

poly(carbonates) Transparent **polymers** which have resistance to heat and other chemicals. They are used in safety spectacles, lenses, and babys' bottles.

poly(chloroethene) (PVC) A **polymer** is made from chloroethene (CH_2=CHCl). PVC has a wide range of uses: vinyl flooring, food containers, fibres, guttering, bottles, windows and cables.

poly(chloroethene)

polyesters Synthetic **polymers** which contain an **ester** group of **atoms**. They are *condensation* polymers whose **monomers** are an **acid** and an **alcohol**.

Polyesters are mainly used to produce **fibres** (80%), film (7%) and packaging materials (10%).

Polyester fibre is used to produce clothing, sometimes blended with other fibres such as **wool**. Because it is a good **insulator**, it is used as a filling for anoraks and duvets. The fibres are also used in car tyres and hoses to give strength.

Polyester film and sheeting is used for videotapes, photographic films and insulating tape. Modern developments include its use in bottles to hold carbonated drinks.

polyesters

poly(ethene)   A **polymer** is made from **ethene** and is usually known as *polythene*.

Poly(ethene) is an **addition polymer**. Here, n is a very large number (about 50 000). Poly(ethene) is widely used today. The polymer is a **saturated alkane** and so is very unreactive.

Poly(ethene) is produced in a *low density* (LDPE) and a *high density* (HDPE) form. LDPE is made into film for packaging, and HDPE is blow-moulded to produce containers such as bottles for washing-up liquid, and pipes and gutters. Both forms can be used to make food boxes and bowls by the injection moulding process.

The **monomer**, ethene, is produced by **cracking** the products of **petroleum** refining, e.g. **naphtha** and **ethane**.

poly(ethene)

polymers Large **molecules** in which a group of atoms are repeated. For example:

$$-x-x-x-x-x-x-x-x-$$
or
$$-x-y-x-y-x-y-x-y-$$

Polymers can be naturally occurring or **synthetic**. **Starch** and **cellulose** are natural, whilst **nylon**, **terylene**, **poly(choroethene)** and **poly(propene)** are synthetic.

Polymers are made by reacting **monomer** molecules together usually with a **catalyst**.

Addition polymerization involves one kind of unsaturated molecule. In the **polymerization** a long chain of atoms (linked by **single bonds**) is formed. See **poly(ethene)**. Because the polymer is a **saturated** molecule it is usually fairly *un*reactive and this gives the polymer useful properties. See the entries for individual polymers.

Condensation polymerization involves two molecules (the monomers) which condense together into long chains. A small molecule is eliminated

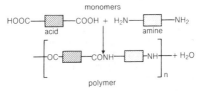

monomer (acrylonitrile)

polymer Addition polymerization used to make fabrics such as Acrilans.

monomers

$$HOOC—\boxed{}—COOH + H_2N—\boxed{}—NH_2$$

acid   amine

$$\left[-OC—\boxed{}—CONH—\boxed{}—NH-\right]_n + H_2O$$

polymer

polymers Condensation polymerization.

during the reaction. The monomers are difunctional molecules, i.e. each molecule possesses two functional groups. **Nylon** and **terylene** are good examples of condensation polymers. Nylon is made by reacting an **acid** and an amine:

The source of most of the raw materials used in making polymers is **petroleum**. There has been great growth in the industry in recent years and will no doubt continue as long as petroleum or a substitute is available.

polymerization The reaction of **monomers** to form a **polymer**.

poly(methylmethacrylate) An **addition polymer** which is transparent. It is stronger than **glass** but easier to scratch and is used widely as a substitute for glass. It is also used to produce baths, car light clusters and aircraft windows. 'Perspex' is a common trade name.

polypeptide A **molecule** which is made up of up to 50 **amino acids** linked together with peptide links. If there are more than 50 amino acids the molecule is termed a **protein**. Polypeptides are important molecules in the body; for example acting as **enzymes**.

poly(phenylethene) (or polystyrene) This is a **polymer** based on the **alkene** phenylethene. It is an addition polymer and is used widely in the form of sheets, mainly in an *expanded* form. Here **air** is blown into the polymer and the result is a white granular **solid** which has excellent **insulation properties**. It is used for cups, ceiling tiles and other items which need to be poor **conductors** of heat. It is also a useful packaging material.

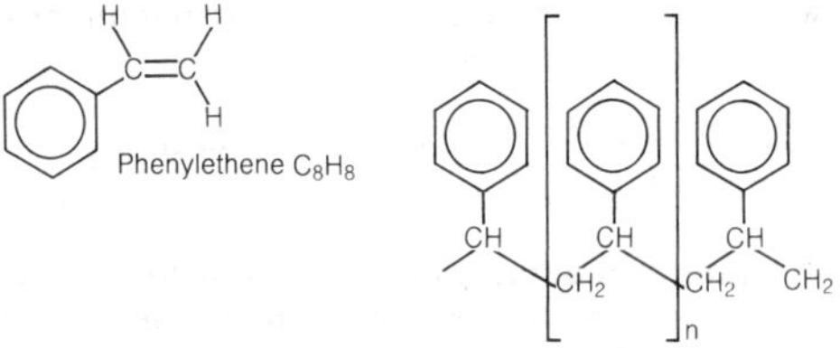

Phenylethene C_8H_8

poly(phenylethene)

poly(propene) A **polymer** similar to **poly(ethene)** in that it is an addition polymer produced from an **alkene**. The alkene is **propene** (C_3H_6) which is obtained from **petroleum**. The polymer is versatile and useful. It is strong and

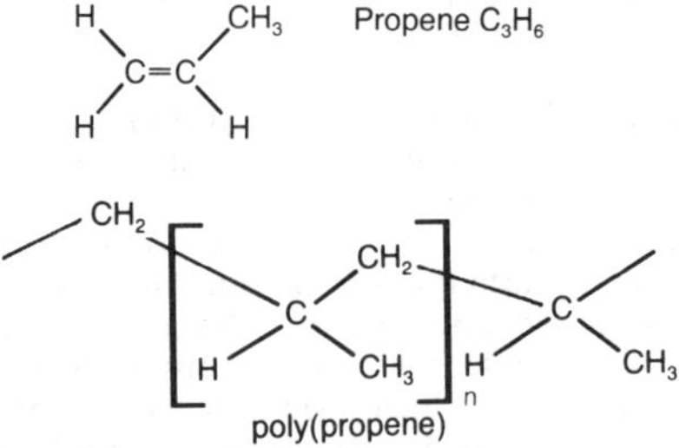

Propene C_3H_6

poly(propene)

hard wearing and finds use as carpet fibres and material for laboratory flasks and beakers. When injection moulded poly(propene) can be made into a wide range of everyday objects such as washing up bowls and car bumpers. It is very unreactive. It is also known as *polypropylene*.

polysaccharides Polymers made up of **sugar** molecules such as **glucose**. There are three common naturally occurring examples:
(a) **Starch**;
(b) **Cellulose**;
(c) Glycogen.
These three are all made up of glucose **molecules** in chains.

Polylsaccharides can be broken down by **hydrolysis** into simple sugars such as glucose or into **disaccharides** such as **maltose**. Hydrolysis is brought about by **enzymes** in plants and animals but can also be done by the use of **acids**.

Polysaccharides are valuable foods, e.g. **starch** in the form of potatoes or rice; **cellulose** is found in all plants and glycogen is the form in which excess **carbohydrate** is stored in animals.

polystyrene See **poly(phenylethene)**.

poly(tetrafluoroethene) (PTFE) Polytetrafluoroethene. This **polymer** is *very* inert. It is the non-stick surface for saucepans, e.g. *Teflon*, *Fluon*. It is also used for bearings and replace-

ment joints in the body because it has a low co-
efficient of friction.

poly(tetrafluoroethene)

polythene See **poly(ethene)**. The older term
'polythene' is still used in industry and shops.

polyurethanes See **urethanes**.

porous Used to describe a material containing
minute passages (*pores*) through which fluids can
pass.

potassium A group I metal. It is a grey, very
soft **element** which is very reactive. It is easily
cut with a knife revealing a silvery surface which
tarnishes immediately. It is a powerful **reducing
agent**, giving rise to the potassium ion (K^+):

$$2K(s) + 2H_2O(l) \rightarrow 2KOH(aq) + H_2(g)$$

It is stored under **oil** because of its reactivity
towards **air** and **water**. The **metal ion** gives a
lilac **flame** test. Potassium is obtained by the
electrolysis of molten potassium chloride (KCl).

potassium compounds Colourless, crystalline
compounds which are very **soluble** in water.

Potassium **salts** play an important role in the body.

Potassium iodide KI	The **solution** is a useful **solvent** for **iodine** forming $KI_3(aq)$. This is used to test for **starch**.
Potassium nitrate KNO_3	*Saltpetre*. Used in food preservation and in explosives.
Potassium manganate(VII) $KMnO_4$	A vivid purple crystalline compound which is a good **oxidizing agent**.

ppt   See **precipitate**.

precipitate (ppt)   The insoluble substance formed on mixing the two **solutions** in a **double decomposition** reaction. For example:

$$Pb(NO_3)_2(aq) + 2NaCl(aq) \rightarrow$$
$$PbCl_2(s) + NaNO_3(aq)$$

$$BaCl_2(aq) + Na_2SO_4(aq) \rightarrow$$
$$BaSO_4(s) + 2NaCl(aq)$$

In these examples, **lead**(II) chloride and barium sulphate are the precipitates.

pressure   A measure of the force pressing onto an object's surface. The **SI unit** of pressure is the **pascal**. Other units used are **atmospheres** and **mmHg**.

The pressure that a **gas** exerts upon its container is caused by **molecules** striking the container's walls. The pressure of a gas depends upon its **volume** and its temperature. See **Boyle's law**, **Charles' law**, **gas laws**.

propane An **alkane** which is obtained from **petroleum**. It is chiefly used as a **fuel**:

$$C_3H_8(g) + 5O_2(g) \rightarrow 3CO_2(g) + 4H_2O(g)$$

Although a **gas** at **room temperature**, it is easily liquified and it is sold as bottled gas, e.g. *Calor Gas* or *Camping Gaz* where it is mixed with **butane**.

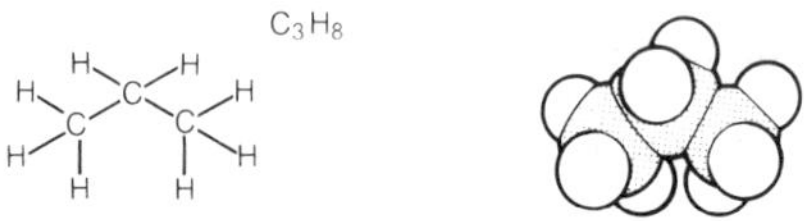

C_3H_8

propane

propene **Hydrocarbon** gas with formula C_3H_6. Propene is an **alkene** which is the **monomer** of the important **polymer, poly(propene)**.

properties The characteristic ways in which a substance behaves (reacts) and which make it what it is and make it different from other substances.

It is usual to classify properties as *physical* or *chemical*. Chemical properties are concerned with the substances' reactions.

Physical properties	Chemical properties
Colour	Whether the substance is a metal or
Density	**non-metal**;
Physical state	Gives acidic or basic oxides;
Boiling point	Has more than one valency;
Melting point	Reacts with acids;
Crystal form	Is an oxidizing or reducing agent
Solubility	
Hardness	

proteins Large, **organic** compounds made up of **chains** of **amino acids**. The **amino acids** are joined by **peptide** links. They are widespread in animal bodies: skin, hair, nail, wool, gristle, muscle.

Proteins form a vital part of our diet. Good sources are: meat, nuts, fish, eggs, milk, cheese, beans, bread. The **enzymes** which play so important a role in living organisms are made up of protein molecules. Animals obtain the food which they need in order to make proteins in their bodies by eating other animals or plants. Plants *make* proteins from the **nitrogen**-containing compounds in the soil. See **fertilizer**.

proton A positively charged **subatomic**

particle found in the **nucleus** of the **atom**. The number of protons in an atom is the same as the **atomic number. Isotopes** of any element *always* contain the same number of protons.

PTFE See **poly(tetrafluoroethene)**.

pure Containing only one **element** or **compound**. For example, sodium chloride crystals can be obtained in a pure state, but table salt is impure because it is mixed with other substances.

PVC (polyvinylchloride) See **poly(chloroethene)**.

pyrites An **ore** of **iron**. Its **formula** is FeS_2 and the **mineral** has a characteristic **brass** colour.

pyrolysis The decomposition of a substance by the action of heat:

$$CaCO_3(s) \rightarrow CaO(s) + CO_2(g)$$

qualitative Describes a statement or **analysis** concerned with composition, not with amounts. For example, water is a **compound** of **hydrogen** and **oxygen**.

quantitative Describes a statement or **analysis** concerned with amounts. For example, water consists of two **atoms** of **hydrogen** and one of **oxygen**.

quartz The transparent **mineral** form of **silica** (silicon oxide SiO_2) which is used in optical instruments such as microscopes and spectroscopes. More **u.v. radiation** passes through quartz than through **glass**.

quicklime The old name for calcium oxide (CaO).

radical In **inorganic chemistry**, the **atom** or **group** of **atoms** present in a **compound** which is responsible for the characteristic **properties** of that compound. For example:

$-SO_4^{2-}$	sulphate
$-CO_3^{2-}$	carbonate
$-OH^-$	hydroxide

radioactive See **radioactivity**.

radioactivity The spontaneous disintegration of the **nucleus** of an **atom** accompanied by the emission of electromagnetic radiation (**gamma rays**) or particles (**alpha** or **beta particles**).

Not all **elements** have radioactive **isotopes**, though many can now be created artificially. Some radioactivity occurs naturally, e.g. isotopes found within rocks. **Granite** usually has quite a large concentration. Living things contain radioactive **carbon** and this can be used for finding the age of their remains (see **radiocarbon dating**). Types of emissions which accompany radio-

active decay include the following:
(a) **Electrons** (beta particles) can be emitted.
(b) Alpha particles can be emitted.
(c) Gamma rays can be emitted.
See **nuclear reactions, half-life**.

radiocarbon dating A technique for determining the age of organic material. **Carbon**-14 (^{14}C) is a naturally occurring radioactive **isotope**. All living things contain ^{14}C, kept at a constant level by continuous exchange through feeding and **respiration**. This exchange ceases on death and the ^{14}C level falls at a constant rate owing to radioactive decay. Scientists measure the amount of radioactivity left in remains, and from this can calculate the age of the remains. See **half-life**.

rate of reaction The rate (or speed) at which a reaction occurs depends on several factors:
(a) *Temperature*: The higher the **temperature**, the faster the reaction is because the particles are moving with greater energies.
(b) *Particle size*: The smaller the particles involved, the greater the surface area where the reaction can take place and the faster is the reaction.
(c) *Concentration*: The more **concentrated** a **solution** (or the higher the **pressure** of a **gas**) the faster a reaction will occur. This is

because there are more particles in a given volume to react.

(d) *Catalysts*: These change the rate by providing an alternative reaction pathway along which the reaction can occur.

raw materials Materials used as the starting point in the production on chemicals or manufactured goods. The major raw materials used in the UK chemical industry are:

(a) **Hydrocarbons**;

(b) **Air**;

(c) **Metallic ores**;

(d) **Minerals**;

(e) **Water**.

For example, the raw material in the production of chlorine is **rock salt** which is then dissolved in water and electrolysed. In the production of **ammonia**, the raw materials used in the UK are **natural gas** and **air**.

rayon One of the first **synthetic** fibres although it is made from a natural material. It is made from **cellulose** (from wood). Wood contains cellulose fibres but they are too short to spin into yarn. Cellulose is dissolved in sodium hydroxide/carbon disulphide solution and squirted into dilute **sulphuric acid**. Here the cellulose is reformed as long threads which are ready for weaving. Rayon is used to make clothes and curtaining.

reaction A change in which one or more chemical **elements** or **compounds** (the *reactants*) form new compounds (the *products*). The product will have different properties from the reactants. Reactions can be accompanied by heat, light sound and colour changes.

reaction types Types of chemical **reaction**. There are many different kinds and include: **addition, dehydration, displacement, dissociation, hydration, hydrolysis, neutralization, polymerization, redox, substitution**.

reactivity series This is a series of **elements** arranged in order of their chemical reactivity.

Potassium
Sodium
Calcium
Magnesium
Aluminium
Zinc
Iron
Lead
Copper
Silver

The series shown here is a short one containing only a few elements but the same general conclusions apply. **Oxides** will be *reduced* by **elements** above them but not the other way round:

$$Mg(s) + CuO(s) \rightarrow MgO(s) + Cu(s)$$

$$Cu(s) + MgO(s) \;-\; \text{no reaction}$$

$$Cu(s) + ZnO(s) \;-\; \text{no reaction}$$

Metal ions will be *reduced* by elements above them but not the other way round:

$$Zn(s) + 2Ag^+(aq) \rightarrow Zn^{2+}(aq) + 2Ag(s)$$

$$Ag(s) + Zn^{2+}(aq) \;-\; \text{no reaction}$$

The higher you go up the series, the more vigorous is the reaction with **water** or **acids**.

Potassium reacts violently with cold water, **magnesium** reacts *very* slowly with cold water but vigorously with **steam**. **Copper** reacts with neither. The **electrochemical series** also involves **non-metals**.

recrystallization A process for the purification of impure crystalline substances. They are dissolved in a **solvent**, filtered, and then allowed to crystallize. In this way impurities are removed.

recycled Used once and is being used again. There is an increasing emphasis on recycling as **resources** become scarce and expensive. Recycling saves **energy** costs and usually makes a country less dependent upon imported goods. **Paper, glass, steel** and **aluminium** are examples of materials which can easily be **recycled**.

redox A **reaction** involving both *red*uction and *ox*idation. Any reaction which involves an

oxidation must also involve a **reduction**.

$$\overset{\text{oxidation}}{\underset{\text{reduction}}{Mg(s) + CuO(s) \rightarrow MgO(s) + Cu(s)}}$$

$$\overset{\text{oxidation}}{\underset{\text{reduction}}{Cu^{2+}(aq) + Zn(s) \rightarrow Cu(s) + Zn^{2+}(aq)}}$$

redox   Examples of reactions.

reducing agent   A chemical that brings about the **reduction** of a substance. In the reaction it itself is always oxidized. Common reducing agents are:

Hydrogen	H_2
Carbon	C
Carbon monoxide	CO
Sulphur dioxide	SO_2
Hydrogen sulphide	H_2S

Reducing agents at work:

$$Fe_2O_3(s) + 3CO(g) \rightarrow 2Fe(l) + 3CO_2(g)$$

$$CuO(s) + H_2(g) \rightarrow Cu(s) + H_2O(g)$$

$$ZnO(s) + C(s) \rightarrow Zn(s) + CO(g)$$

reduction   A substance undergoes reduction if it:

(a) loses **oxygen** $PbO(s) + C(s) \rightarrow Pb(s) + CO$

(b) gains **hydrogen** $Cl_2(g) + H_2(g) \rightarrow 2HCl(g)$

(c) gains **electrons** $Na^+(l) + e^- \rightarrow Na(l)$

See **oxidation, reducing agent, redox**.

refining A process for either the removal of impurities from a substance or the removal of components from a mixture.

(a) **Metals.** When a metal has been extracted from its ores it is often not in a pure state. For some uses this might be acceptable, e.g. pig iron contain impurities. Other uses demand a purer product and then the metal is refined until the right purity is achieved.

(b) **Petroleum.** A complex **mixture** of **hydrocarbons**. To make it more useful it is first of all split up into separate parts. These parts are known as *fractions* and the separation is done by fractional distillation. The fractions are also mixtures but are not so complicated. They contain compounds whose **boiling points** are within a certain range.

Conditions vary from refinery to refinery and depend on what products are required. The major product might be **petrol** or it might be petrochemical feedstock which is then turned into **alkenes**, etc. for the production of polymers. See **cracking, reforming**.

reforming An important process which is used in **petroleum** refineries and chemical plants. **Molecules** are taken and altered into more useful products. There is no change in the size of the molecule. One example is the conversion of unbranched **alkanes** into branched ones, these giving **petrol** a higher **octane rating**:

octane   2-methylheptane

Another example is the production of **aromatic** compounds from **alkenes**:

$$C_7H_{14} \rightarrow \quad C_7H_8 + 3H_2$$

heptene   **methylbenzene** hydrogen

refractory materials Materials which do not either melt or change in any way below 1500°C and which can be used as furnace linings. Examples include **china clay**, silica, alumina, **bauxite**.

relative atomic mass (RAM) The **mass** of an 'average atom' of an **element** compared with an atom of the $^{12}_{6}C$ **carbon isotope** which is given the value of exactly 12. see A_r.

relative molecular mass (RMM) See M_r.

residue The waste product remaining after any chemical process is complete.

respiration The process by which **energy** is

obtained by plants and animals. In animals, food is eaten and broken down in the body. **Oxygen** is breathed in by taking **air** into the lungs. The oxygen is carried round the body in the blood. **Reactions** occur between the oxygen and the broken-down food and heat is released. **Carbon dioxide** is also produced and this is breathed out. The waste products from the food are excreted from the body. The energy released is used for heat, movement, growth and all other body functions.

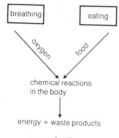

respiration

reversible reactions Reactions that can go in either direction, depending on the conditions that exist. For example:

$$Fe_2O_3(s) + 3H_2(g) \rightleftharpoons 2Fe(s) + 3H_2O(g)$$

Steam can react with hot **iron** or **hydrogen** can reduce iron (III) oxide. In both cases, an **equilibrium** will exist with all four substances present unless the products are removed.

rock cycle The change over long periods of time (millions of years) as rocks on Earth change from one kind to another. This is also known as the *geochemical cycle*. See **sedimentary** rock, **igneous** rock, **metamorphic** rock, **Earth** structure.

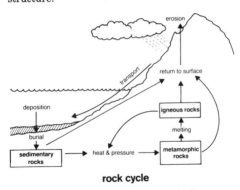

rock cycle

rock salt Impure crystalline deposits of **sodium chloride**. The **solid** is purified before use.

room temperature A temperature of between 15°C and 25°C. It is not a fixed temperature, but is a range.

rubber A natural **polymer**. It is a **hydrocarbon** and its structure is shown here:

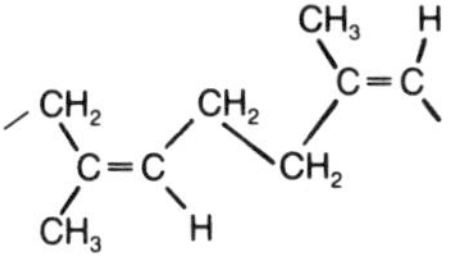

Today most 'rubber' is made from butadiene:

$$(CH_2 = CH - CH = CH_2)$$

by **polymerization**. Rubber is elastic and a good **insulator**. Its uses are widespread from tyres and gloves to waterproofing.

rust The reddish-brown product of corrosion of **iron** which has been exposed to **air** and **water**. It is hydrated iron(III) oxide ($Fe_2O_3 . xH_2O$). Rusting is of great economic importance. It is most commonly prevented by coating the iron with **paint**, **plastic** or another **metal**. See **electroplating**, **galvanizing**.

sacrificial anode A reactive **metal** which is attached to another metal or **alloy** which needs protection from **oxidation**. For example, bars of

zinc are welded to undersea pipelines so that the more reactive zinc will oxidize in preference to the less reactive iron. In this way the steel of the pipeline is protected. **Galvanizing** is another example of this process. See **anode**.

salt A **compound** formed when the **hydrogen** of an **acid** is totally or partially replaced by a metal, e.g.:

$$Zn(s) + HCl(aq) \rightarrow ZnCl_2(aq) + H_2(g)$$

When an acid reacts with a **base** the products are a salt and **water** only:

$$NaOH(aq) + HNO_3(aq) \rightarrow NaNO_3(aq) + H_2O(l)$$

Salts can also be made by direct combination of two elements:

$$2Na(s) + Cl_2(g) \rightarrow 2NaCl(s)$$

With a **dibasic acid**, if only one hydrogen **atom** is replaced, the result is an **acid salt**.

sand A **mixture** of fine particles of **rock** fragments. Sand is widely found on Earth and is extensively used as a building material. It contains a high proportion of **silica** (SiO_2).

sandstone A common **sedimentary** rock.

saponification The process of the **hydrolysis** of an **ester** when *alkaline* conditions are used. The breakdown of natural fats to produce soap is an example of saponification. Here sodium hydroxide **solution** is used to produce an **alcohol** and the **sodium salt** of the **carboxylic acid (soap)**. See **detergent**.

saturated compound An **organic** compound containing *only* **single bonds**. **Compounds** which contain **double** or **triple bonds** are said to be **unsaturated**. Examples include ethane and butan-1-ol.

saturated solution A **solution** which contains the maximum amount of **solute** at a given temperature in the presence of excess **solute**. The amount of solute needed to form a saturated solution depends on the **temperature**. The only way of putting more solute into a saturated solution is by changing the temperature. See **supersaturated solution**.

sedimentary rock Rock formed from *sediments* — solid materials — which have been laid down in the sea over millions of years. As the layers of materials build up, the pressure increases and the particles are compressed to form a new rock. Most of the Earth's crust is covered by a thin layer of sedimentary rocks.

The original sediments are formed from materials such as **sand**, gravel and mud produced by the action of weather on existing rocks. Examples of sedimentary rocks are **sandstone**, **limestone**, **chalk**. See **rock cycle**.

semiconductor An electrical **conductor** with unusual **properties**. As the **temperature** increases or the substance contains greater amounts of impurity the resistance of the material *decreases*. In practice, when **crystals** of semiconductors are grown, controlled amounts of impurity are added to obtain *exactly* the properties which are required.

Substances which have semiconduction properties can be **elements** or **compounds** but usually involve *metalloids*. Examples include: gallium, germanium, **arsenic**.

separation of mixtures Mixtures can be separated if the substances in the mixture have different physical **properties**. Which technique is used depends on the mixture. Techniques include: filtration, **fractional distillation**, **chromatography**, decantation.

sewage treatment Waste water from industry or the home is treated in several ways in order to make it fit again for use:
(a) The material is passed through a screen to remove large solid objects and **sand** and grit

are allowed to settle out.

(b) It is then passed through settling tanks where small particles sink to form a sludge; this sludge is treated with bacteria and the **methane** formed can be collected and used. The treated sludge can be used as a **fertilizer**.

(c) The remaining **liquid** is then treated in one of two ways:

(i) it is sprayed over a bed of coke which contains bacteria; these digest any organic material which remains;

(ii) it is mixed with micro-organisms and churned up by having air passed through it; again, the organic material is digested.

(d) The remaining liquid is then ready for discharge into rivers.

shell   See **electronic configuration**.

SI units   An international system of **units** based on the metric system of measurement.

Quantity	Unit	Symbol
Length	metre	m
Mass	kilogramme	kg
Time	second	s
Current	ampère	A
Temperature	kelvin	K
Amount of substance	mole	mol
Luminous intensity	candela	cd

There are seven basic units and the system is used in scientific and technological work throughout the world.

silica A widely found **mineral** form of silicon oxide (SiO_2) which is used as an **ore** of **silicon**. Some silica is found as coloured crystals, e.g. amethyst (containing the Fe^{3+} **ion**); other forms of silica include *flint*, which is an **amorphous** form.

silicon A **group** IV **metalloid**. It is a very abundant **element**, the second most abundant in the earth's crust (27.7%), being a part of the chemical composition of many rocks. It is a **semiconductor** and is the heart of micro-electronic technology in the form of the silicon chip. Silicon is found naturally in the form of metal silicates and silica (silicon dioxide). The **mineral**, **quartz**, is the purest form of silica. **Sand** is tiny **crystals** of silica with various impurities.

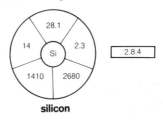

silicon

silk Fibres of natural **protein**, from the cocoons of the silk moth, which are fine and very flexible. Silk fibres can be spun to produce yarns which are strong, soft and shiny. Silk is used to produce expensive but hard-wearing materials.

silver A **transition metal**. It is used for jewellery and decorative purposes and has been used for coinage. It is often alloyed with **copper** to give strength. It is an excellent **conductor** of electricity and heat. When exposed to the **air** it slowly becomes covered in a black film of silver sulphide.

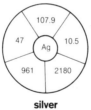

107.9

47

10.5

Ag

961

2180

silver

Silver is low in the **reactivity series**. Its **oxide** is unstable:

$$\begin{array}{c} \text{heat} \\ Ag_2O(s) \rightarrow 2Ag(s) + O_2(g) \end{array}$$

Its **halides** are also unstable. This property is used in photography:

$$\text{light}$$
$$2AgBr(s) \rightarrow 2Ag(s) + Br_2(g)$$

See **photochemical reactions**.

single bond   A **covalent bond** which is made up of a shared pair of **electrons**. Examples are found in all **organic** compounds and in **compounds** formed from **non-metals**.

slag   A **mixture** of molten **oxides** produced during the **smelting** and **refining** of **ores**. Slag plays an important part in these processes because it dissolves impurities from the ores and keeps them separate from the liquid **metal**. To help this process, materials are added which reduce the **melting point** of the oxide mixture. **Limestone** is a good example. Examples of impurities which are removed during **steel manufacture** include **carbon**, **phosphorus** and **sulphur**. Solid slags are used for a variety of purposes which include **cement** production.

slaked lime   The common name for **calcium hydroxide** $(Ca(OH)_2)$. It can be produced by adding **water** to **lime**, known as *slaking*:

$$CaO(s) + H\ O(l) \rightarrow Ca(OH)\ (s)$$

A **solution** of slaked lime in water is known as **limewater**. Slaked lime is used in agriculture and in making **mortar**. See **calcium compounds**, **limestone**.

smelting A process of extracting metals which involves melting the **ore**.

soap A cleaning agent which is made by the action of an **alkali**, e.g. sodium hydroxide solution, on naturally occurring esters. See **saponification**.

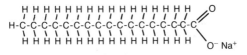

soap A soapy detergent molecule.

The **hydrocarbon** end of the **molecule** is **hydrophobic**. The carboxylate end of the molecule is **hydrophilic**.

Soap is made from a mixture of animal **fat**, and vegetable **oils** such as coconut oil. An **antioxidant** is usually added to prevent the soap from producing 'off' smells. Soap is **biodegradable**. See **detergent**.

sodium A soft, grey **metal** which is in **group** I of the **periodic table**. It is easily cut with a knife revealing a silvery surface which rapidly tarnishes. It is stored under **oil** because of its

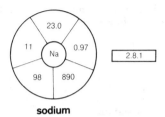

sodium

reactivity towards **air** and **water**. It is very reactive towards water and **non-metals**, e.g.

$$Na(s) + 2H_2O(l) \rightarrow NaOH(aq) + H_2(g)$$

$$2Na(s) + Cl_2(g) \rightarrow 2NaCl(s)$$

The metal **ion** gives a yellow/orange **flame test**.

Sodium is extracted from molten **sodium chloride** by **electrolysis**:

$$2NaCl(l) \rightarrow 2Na(l) + Cl_2(g)$$

The sodium chloride is obtained by mining **rock salt**. Sodium metal is used as a coolant in fast-breeder nuclear reactors (see **nuclear reaction**) and in the manufacture of the **petrol** additive tetraethyl lead ($Pb(C_2H_5)_4$) which is used to raise the octane rating of fuels. It is also used to produce **biocides**, pharmaceuticals and **catalysts**, and to extract metals, e.g. titanium:

$$TiCl_4(l) + 4Na(l) \rightarrow Ti(s) + 4NaCl(l)$$

Sodium ions (Na⁺) are an important constituent of the fluids in animal tissues.

sodium compounds

Sodium carbonate Na_2CO_3	Compound made in the **Solvay process** and an important chemical. One of its many uses is in the manufacture of **glass**.
	Unlike most carbonates, it is **soluble** in water. It is not decomposed by heat, its aqueous **solution** is alkaline.
Sodium chloride NaCl	Known as *common salt*. Obtained from *rock salt* and is used to make **sodium hydroxide**, **sodium metal** and **chloride**. It is used for flavouring and preserving foods. See **Solvay process**.
Sodium hydrogen-carbonate $NaHCO_3$	Used in **baking powder**. It is decomposed by the action of heat or **acids**.
	Also used in fire extinguishers and in anti-indigestion powders.
Sodium hydroxide NaOH	Produced by the **electrolysis** of **brine** and has wide uses in industry, e.g. making **soap**, fibres such as **rayon** and **paper**. It is a **caustic alkali**. Solutions have pH >10.

Sodium nitrate $NaNO_3$	Used as a **fertilizer** and in the preservation of meat. Usually forms part of the **mixture** of *salts* used in **curing** meats such as bacon, gammon and corned beef.
Sodium thiosulphate $Na_2S_2O_3$	Compound used in the photographic process. It is used to *fix* the negative and is often known as *hypo*. It reacts with unreacted silver bromide and therefore makes sure that no further reaction with light occurs.

softboard Material made from small wood chippings which are heated and then passed between two rollers to form a spongy board. Softboard has good sound **insulation** properties and is often used for notice boards. See **chipboard**.

softening See **hardness of water**.

solder A fusible **alloy** used for bonding **metals**. It is usually an **alloy** of **tin** and **lead** in various proportions, depending upon the use.

solid A substance whose **atoms** or **molecules** are fixed in positions and do not have the freedom of movement found in a **liquid** or a **gas**. Atoms and molecules are held in a **lattice** by **bonds**. It is only when these bonds are broken that the atoms and molecules are able to move and the solid melts. See **melting**.

As **heat energy** is put into the solid lattice the atoms or molecules acquire enough energy to break the bonds. Although the atoms or molecules within the lattice do not move from place to place they do vibrate.

soluble Describes a substance able to **dissolve** in a **solvent**. The extent to which any **solute** dissolves depends on the solvent and the **temperature**. At any given temperature there is a maximum amount of solute which can dissolve in a fixed **volume** of solvent. This produces a **saturated solution**. See solubility.

solubility The extent to which a **solute** in a **solvent** will **dissolve**. An **ionic** substance will have a higher solubility in a **polar** solvent than a covalently bonded solute, e.g. **copper(II) sulphate** is much more soluble in **water** than is **methane**. The **units** used are **moles** of solute in 100 g of solvent at a *stated temperature*, although other units, e.g. mole/**dm**^{3}, g/100 g, are also used.

solute Any substance which **dissolves** in a **solvent** to produce a **solution**, e.g. when **copper(II) sulphate** dissolves in **water** to produce a solution, copper(II) sulphate is the solute.

solution The liquid mixture resulting when a

solid, liquid or gas **dissolves** in a **solvent**. In a solution, the particles of the **solute** (i.e. its **atoms** or **molecules**) are spread throughout the body of the solvent and are not visible.

Solvay process The process by which cheap **raw materials** (**brine** and **calcium carbonate** — **limestone**) are turned into the valuable alkali, **sodium carbonate**. For example:

$$2NaCl(aq) + CaCO_3(s) \rightarrow$$
$$CaCl_2(aq) + Na_2CO_3(aq)$$

Because both sodium carbonate and calcium chloride are soluble in **water**, the **reaction** shown cannot be carried out *directly*. It does work, however, by a series of steps:
(a) Limestone is heated:

$$CaCO_3(s) \rightarrow CaO(s) + CO_2(g)$$

(b) Ammonia is dissolved in brine ($NaCl + NH_3$).
(c) Carbon dioxide (produced from the limestone) is passed into the brine/ammonia solution. The following reaction occurs:

$$NaCl(aq) + CO_2(g) + NH_3(g) + H_2O(l) \rightarrow$$
$$NaHCO_3(s) + NH_4Cl(aq)$$

Sodium hydrogencarbonate is produced because of its low **solubility**. It can be removed from the mixture.
(d) Sodium carbonate is produced by heating the

hydrogencarbonate:

$$2NaHCO_3(s) \rightarrow Na_2CO_3(s) + H_2O(l) + CO_2(g)$$

(e) In the final stage the ammonia is recovered from the ammonium chloride:

$$2NH_4Cl(aq) + CaO(s) \rightarrow$$
$$CaCl_2(aq) + 2NH_3(g) + H_2O(l)$$

The ammonia and carbon dioxide produced in these last two stages are recycled and used again. The only **by-product** of the reaction is calcium chloride ($CaCl_2$).

solvent A **liquid** in which a **solute dissolves** to form a **solution**. **Water** is the most common solvent. Solvents may be polar, e.g. water, or non-polar, e.g. **ether**. Polar solvents dissolve in ionic or polar solutes, e.g. **salts**. Non-polar solvents dissolve **covalent** molecules, e.g. **hydrocarbons**.

spectator ions Ions which play no part in a **reaction**. They are only *spectators*. In the example shown below the spectator ions are underlined.

$$\underline{Na^+(aq)} + Cl^-(aq) + Ag^+(aq) + \underline{NO_3^-(aq)} \rightarrow$$
$$\underline{Na^+(aq)} + \underline{NO_3^-(aq)} + AgCl(s)$$

The **ionic equation** for this reaction is

$$Ag^+(aq) + Cl^-(aq) \rightarrow AgCl(s)$$

stalactites, stalagmites Mineral growths found in caves. When **water** containing **calcium salts** falls into the cave there is a gradual build up of **calcium carbonate** from the roof (forming stalactites) and onto the floor (forming stalagmites) as the **solution** containing the calcium salts decomposes.

$$Ca(HCO_3)_2(aq) \rightarrow CaCO_3(s) + H_2O(l) + CO_2(g)$$

starch (($C_6H_{10}O_5)_n$)) A **carbohydrate polymer**. It is made up of glucose **monomers** and can be broken down by the action of **enzymes** or dilute **acid**. **Glucose** or **maltose** is formed. Starch is insoluble in **water** and is a white tasteless powder. It is found in most plants and is used by plants as a food. Animals also use it as food when they eat plants, e.g. potatoes, rice, flour.

In the presence of starch, **iodine** solution turns blue. This can be used as a test for iodine or starch. See **polysaccharide**.

states of matter The way substances exist. There are three states of matter: **solid**, **liquid** and **gas**. Substances are changed from one state into another by altering the **temperature**. See **change of state**.

state symbols The letters placed next to the

formula of a substance, usually in brackets, in a chemical **equation** to denote the **state of matter** of that substance in the reaction. They are: (s)=**solid**, (l)=**liquid**, (g)=**gas**, (aq)=**aqueous solution**.

steam Water vapour above its **boiling point**. Steam is a colourless **gas**. The 'steam' which is seen coming from a kettle is normally *below* the boiling point and is made up of droplets of water which have cooled and condensed. See **condensation**.

steel An **alloy** which contains **iron** as the main constituent. Depending on which other **elements** are present, substances of varying properties can be formed. The two best known steels are *mild steel*, which is used for car bodies and household goods such as cookers, freezers, etc., and *stainless steel*, which is used in industry and in cooking utensils. Mild steel **rusts** easily and so has to be protected by **galvanizing**, enamelling or painting. Stainless steel is not corroded by oxygen and so is very useful. There are many steel alloys. Stainless steel contains:
(a) iron — 74%;
(b) chromium — 18%;
(c) nickel — 8%.
Steel-cutting tools contain tungsten, and high-temperature steels contain molybdenum. See **steel manufacture**.

steel manufacture Steel is made by two methods: the basic oxygen process and the electric arc process.

In the *basic oxygen process*, scrap steel (25% of the total **mass**) and a little **limestone** are dissolved in molten **iron** (which comes straight from the **blast furnace**). Pure **oxygen** is then blown onto the surface of the molten **mixture** and the impurities such as **carbon** are burnt off. Other metals are added to produce steel with the correct composition and, when the process is complete, the steel is cast into long continuous strips. The process is used to produce everyday steels used in heavy engineering, canning, car bodies and household goods.

In the *electric arc process* the **raw material** is solid scrap steel. A large **electric current** is passed through the steel until it melts. Oxygen is used to burn off impurities, and additional materials are added to produce the required composition. The process is used to produce more specialist steels such as stainless and surgical steels.

sterilization A heat-treatment process to reduce the number of micro-organisms present in a substance. This extends the shelf-life of food such as milk which is sterilized in the bottle by being heated to between 115 °C and 130 °C for between 10 and 20 minutes. Sterilized milk can be kept without refrigeration for up to 5 months. Surgical and dental instruments are examples of tools which are kept free from micro-organisms by sterilization. See **pasteurization, UHT**.

STP *Standard Temperature and Pressure.* The conditions it refers to are one **atmosphere pressure** and a **temperature** of 0°C (273 K). When comparing gas **volumes** it is useful to have standard conditions to refer to.

strengths of acids and bases Acids and bases are termed *strong* if they are fully dissociated in **solution** (see **dissociation**). Good examples are acids such as hydrochloric, nitric and sulphuric, and bases such as sodium or potassium hydroxide.

$$HCl(aq) \rightleftharpoons H^+(aq) + Cl^-(aq)$$
$$\text{pH range 1–2}$$
$$NaOH(aq) \rightleftharpoons Na^+(aq) + OH^-(aq)$$
$$\text{pH range 13–14}$$

Weak acids and bases do not fully dissociate in solution. Here the equilibria lie to the left-hand side. Good examples are found in the organic acids, e.g. citric, tartaric, ethanoic and malic; and in bases such as ammonia.

$$CH_3COOH(aq) \rightleftharpoons CH_3COO^-(aq) + H^+(aq)$$
$$\text{pH range 3–6}$$
$$NH_3(aq) + H_2O(l) \rightleftharpoons NH_4^+(aq) + OH^-(aq)$$
$$\text{pH range 8–11}$$

strong acid and base   See **strengths of acids and bases**.

structural formula   A **formula** that shows the **bond** between **atoms** and the position of the atoms with respect to each other. The **molecular formula** shows the number of atoms in the **molecule**. Structural formulae are usually shown as two-dimensional diagrams, even though the molecule may not be **planar**. Examples are:

ethane C_2H_6

ethanol C_2H_5OH

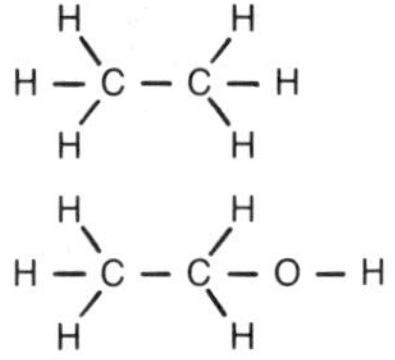

molecular formula   structural formula

subatomic particles   Particles found in the atom. The important ones are the **proton**, **neutron** and **electron**.

sublime   To change directly from a **solid** to a **gas** without first melting. Common substances which sublime are carbon dioxide (CO_2) and iron(II) chloride ($FeCl_2$).

substitution reaction   A reaction where some

atoms or groups in a **molecule** are replaced by others. It is a common reaction of **organic** compounds. For example:

$$CH_4(g) + Cl_2(g) \rightarrow CH_3Cl(l) + HCl(g)$$

A C—H bond is replaced by a C—Cl bond.

sucrose ($C_{12}H_{22}O_{11}$) A **disaccharide** which is made up of a **fructose** unit and a **glucose** unit. It is the white crystalline **sugar** that is used in the home. It is obtained from sugar beet and cane sugar.

sugar The common general term for those sweet compounds which chemically are **monosaccharides** and **disaccharides**. Examples: **glucose**, **sucrose**, **fructose**, **maltose**. See **carbohydrate**.

sulphates Compounds containing the SO_4^{2-} **ion** (**valency**=2). They are widespread in nature, e.g. **gypsum** ($CaSO_4$). They can be produced in the laboratory by the action of **sulphuric acid** on **metals** or **oxides** and **hydroxides**.

The test for a sulphate is to add a **solution** to an acidified (HCl) solution of barium chloride. If a sulphate is present a white **precipitate** is formed which is insoluble in dilute acid.

sulphides Compounds of **sulphur** with

another **element**. They are produced by reaction with **sulphur** or **hydrogen sulphide**:

$$Fe(s) + S(s) \rightarrow FeS(s)$$
$$CuSO_4(aq) + H_2S(g) \rightarrow CuS(s) + H_2SO_4(aq)$$

sulphites Compounds containing the SO_3^{2-} ion. They can be thought of as **salts** of **sulphurous acid** H_2SO_3. **Sulphur(IV) oxide** is prepared in the laboratory by the action of **acid** on a sulphite.

sulphur (S_8) A yellow non-metallic **element** which exists as two allotropic forms. *Rhombic sulphur* is the stable form below 96°C and *monoclinic sulphur* is stable above that temperature. The figures in the chart refer to the monoclinic **allotrope**.

Sulphur is in **group** VI of the **periodic table** and is reactive towards **metals** and **oxygen**. It is found uncombined in nature as well as occurring as metal sulphides, e.g. galena (PbS) and pyrite (FeS).

Sulphur-containing compounds are also found in **petroleum** and **natural gas**, which are now the major sources of the element. Sulphur is an important constituent of some drugs, e.g. sulphonamides, and is used in the manufacture of **agrochemicals** and **dyes**, but its major use is in the manufacture of sulphuric acid in the **contact process**. See **vulcanizing, Frasch process, desulphurization**.

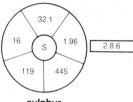

sulphur

sulphur compounds

Sulphur(IV) oxide SO_2	Commonly called **sulphur dioxide** and is a colourless **gas** with a sharp odour. It is produced by burning **sulphur** or sulphur compounds in **air** or **oxygen**. It dissolves in **water** to form **sulphurous acid** — a weak acid. It is useful as a sterilizing agent and is often added to soft drinks. It is a **reducing agent**. This property is used in the chemical test for the gas. Sulphur dioxide is a major cause of air **pollution** and **acid rain**, being produced by the **combustion** of **fossil fuels**.
Sulphur(VI) oxide SO_3	A **volatile solid** with a sharp odour. It is produced in the **contact process** by the combination of sulphur dioxide and oxygen over a **catalyst** (vanadium pentoxide). The oxide is acidic and when it is added to water, **sulphuric acid** is formed.

sulphuric acid (H$_2$SO$_4$) One of the most important chemicals produced. It is a colourless, oily
liquid which is a **strong acid** and a vigorous
oxidizing agent. It is made in the **contact process** and the annual production in the UK is
about 2.5 million **tonnes**. The chart shows the
main uses of the acid and the approximate
amounts of the acid which are used.

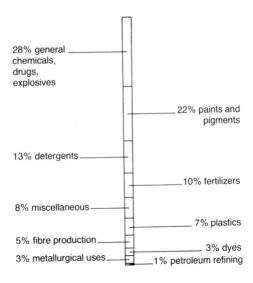

28% general chemicals, drugs, explosives

22% paints and pigments

13% detergents

10% fertilizers

8% miscellaneous

7% plastics

5% fibre production

3% dyes

3% metallurgical uses

1% petroleum refining

Sulphuric acid reacts chemically in several ways.

(a) *As an acid:* dilute sulphuric acid reacts with **metals, bases** and **carbonates** to form sulphates:

$$Mg(s) + H_2SO_4(aq) \rightarrow MgSO_4(aq) + H_2(g)$$

$$CuO(s) + H_2SO_4(aq) \rightarrow CuSO_4(aq) + H_2O(l)$$

Concentrated sulphuric acid reacts with chlorides and nitrates to form hydrogen chloride and nitric acid respectively:

$$H_2SO_4(l) + NaCl(s) \rightarrow NaHSO_4(s) + HCl(g)$$

$$H_2SO_4(l) + NaNO_3(s) \rightarrow NaHSO_4(s) + HNO_3(g)$$

(b) *As a dehydrating agent:* the concentrated acid is **hygroscopic**. Concentrated sulphuric acid is sometimes used to dry gases.

If the concentrated acid is added to **sucrose**, the sugar turns black. This is because water is removed from the **carbohydrate** and **carbon** is left behind:

$$C_6H_{12}O_6(s) \rightarrow 6C(s) + 6H_2O(g)$$

The reaction between concentrated suphuric acid and water is very exothermic. It is important always to add the acid to water and not the other way round.

(c) *As an oxidizing agent:* although copper cannot displace hydrogen from acids, the metal can be oxidized by concentrated sulphuric acid:

$$Cu(s) + 2H_2SO_4(l) \rightarrow CuSO_4(s) + SO_2(g) + 2H_2O(l)$$

sulphurous acid (H_2SO_3) An **acid** which only exists in **aqueous solution**, formed by passing **sulphur dioxide** into **water**.

It is a **weak acid** and a **reducing agent**. When heated, **sulphur dioxide** and **steam** are produced, leaving no residue. **Salts** of the acid are called **sulphites**.

superphosphate A **fertilizer** which is a valuable source of **phosphorus**. Superphosphate is formed by heating (insoluble) **calcium phosphate** and **sulphuric acid** under **pressure**. It is a mixture of calcium dihydrogenphosphate (which is **soluble**), **calcium sulphate** and other **compounds**.

supersaturated solution A **solution** which contains a higher **concentration** of **solute** than a **saturated solution**. It is usually produced by cooling the saturated solution. If the solution is disturbed, e.g. by a mechanical shock, by dust falling into it or by a crystal of the solute being added to it, the excess solute will usually crystallize out. See **crystallization**.

suspension When a **solid** is added to a **liquid** and the solid neither **dissolves** in the liquid nor sinks to the bottom of the vessel, the **mixture** is referred to as a suspension because the solid is *suspended* in the liquid.

symbol In chemistry, usually letters used to *represent* the names of substances. Symbols are also used in representing **units**.

synthesis The production of something from smaller or simpler parts, e.g. of **ammonia** from **hydrogen** and **nitrogen**. See **synthesis gas**.

synthesis gas A **mixture** of **carbon monoxide** and **hydrogen** gas produced by the **steam reforming** of **natural gas** or **naphtha** using a nickel oxide catalyst. There are two steps in the process:

$$CH_4(g) + H_2O(g) \rightarrow 3H_2(g) + CO(g)$$
$$CO(g) + H_2O(g) \rightarrow H_2(g) + CO_2(g)$$

As the name implies, synthesis gas is used to produce other chemicals. It is an important feedstock for the chemical industry. See **methanol**.

synthetic Made from artificial rather than **natural** substances. For example, **nylon** is an artificial **fibre**, **silk** is a natural fibre.

talc The **mineral** form of hydrated magnesium silicate ($Mg_3(OH)_2Si_4O_{10}$) which is used as a lubricant and as a base for dusting powders.

tar Any heavy, thick **liquid** which is produced by the **distillation** (in the absence of **air**) of **carbon**-containing materials such as wood or **coal**. Tars are rich sources of **organic compounds**.

temperature The measure of the **kinetic energy** of a substance. The temperature scale used in everyday life is the Celsius (or centigrade) scale. In scientific work, the **Kelvin** scale is usually used. See **room temperature**.

tempering To strengthen or toughen a metal or metal object by heat treatment, usually by heating it and then quenching it in water or oil. See **annealing**.

temporary hardness See **hardness of water**.

terylene A **polyester** which is widely used in the clothing and household furnishing industries. It is often mixed with **natural fibres**, e.g. terylene/wool mixtures. Its **monomers** are a dialcohol and a diacid.

tetrachloromethane A dense, colourless **liquid** which is **immiscible** with **water**. It is a good **solvent** for non-**polar** compounds. It can be made from **methane** by a **substitution reaction** involving **chlorine**:

$$4Cl_2(g) + CH_4(g) \rightarrow CCl_4(l) + HCl(g)$$

Other substituted methane products are also formed: (CH_3Cl, CH_2Cl_2, $CHCl_3$) and the **mixture** must be separated to obtain **pure** products.

tetrahedral compound   A **compound** in which four **atoms** are arranged as if at the corners of a tetrahedron and linked to an atom at the centre of it by **covalent** or **coordinate bonds**. In a **carbon compound** such as **methane**, where there are four **single bonds** leading to four **atoms**, the atoms are arranged tetrahedrally around the carbon atom. The bonds point to the corners of the imaginary cube that the carbon atom is in the centre of. In this way, the atoms are as far away from each other as possible. The angle between the bonds is 109° 28' — *tetrahedral angle*.

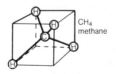

tetrahedral   The bonds in a carbon atom.

thermal 'To do with heat'. For example thermal decomposition is decomposition by heat. Thermal **energy** is **heat energy**.

thermit reaction Whereby aluminium removes the **oxygen** from the **oxide** of a metal *below* it in the **reactivity series**. **Iron**(II) oxide was used in industry to provide a small source of molten metal. Great heat is liberated in the reaction and the products are iron and aluminium oxide.

$$Fe_2O_3(s) + 2Al(s) \rightarrow Al_2O_3(s) + 2Fe(l)$$

thermometer Instrument for measuring **temperature**: how hot something is. Although they come in different forms; the 'liquid in glass' thermometer is common. The liquid — usually **mercury** — is held in a bulb. As the temperature rises, the liquid expands in the bulb and rises up the tube. The tube is marked at intervals with the temperature and this can be read off.

thermoplastic A **polymer** which softens when it is heated and can be moulded and re-moulded into new shapes. Examples are **nylon** and **poly(chloroethene)**.

thermosetting A **polymer** which cannot be softened again once it has been formed. Decomposition occurs if it is heated again. Examples are **bakelite** and formica.

tin A **metal** which is in **group** IV of the **periodic table**. It occurs as **allotropes**, the most common being grey tin and white tin. The grey form is stable at low temperatures and the data given in the diagram refers to the white form. White tin is a shiny metal which shows normal metallic reactions. It is found naturally as the **oxide**, SnO_2

Tin is used to make **tinplate**, **bronze**, **solder** and **alloys** for bearings. It is also used in the production of **glass**. Glass is floated onto the surface of molten tin. In this way large areas of glass without defects are formed.

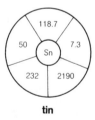

tin

tinplate Mild **steel** which, by **electroplating**, has been given a thin layer of **tin**. Tinplate is used in the canning industry to provide an **inert** layer between the steel of the can and the food.

titanium A **transition metal** which is common in the Earth's crust (0.5%). It forms **alloys** which are very strong while having a low **density**. It is resistant to **corrosion** up to a high **temperature**. Titanium alloys are used in the aircraft industry. TiO$_2$ is used as a **pigment**.

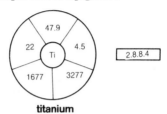

titanium

titration   The reaction of two **solutions** used in **analysis** to discover the **concentration** of one of the solutions. An accurately measured volume of one solution is normally placed in a conical **flask** and the other in a **burette**. The solution from the burette is added slowly until the other solution has been completely used up. This is shown by the use of an **indicator** or by means of a **pH** meter or a conductivity meter. The technique is most commonly used for **acid-base reactions**. See **volumetric analysis**.

tonne   A **unit** of **mass**. One tonne equals 1000 kilogrammes. It is 2205 lb and so is 35 lb lighter than the imperial ton (2240 lb), The tonne (or *metric ton*) is now widely used.

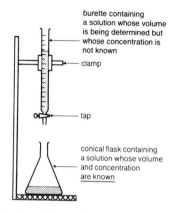

titration Discovering the concentration of a solution.

transition metals The **elements** found in the central section of the **periodic table**. There are three series of them but the most important are those elements from scandium to **zinc**. Transition metals have similar **properties**.

(a) They produce coloured **compounds**.
(b) They have variable **valency**.
(c) They are high **melting** and **boiling point** solids.

(d) They are useful as **catalysts**.

(e) They have **cations** which are useful as catalysts.

They tend to be important elements for use as metals, e.g. **iron, copper, silver, gold, mercury, zinc, platinum**, or for use in **alloys**, e.g. **titanium, vanadium, chromium, manganese, cobalt, nickel**, tungsten.

transition temperature The **temperature** above which one **allotrope** is stable and below which another is stable. Some examples are shown here:

(a) Rhombic sulphur stable *below* 96°C, monoclinic sulphur stable *above* 96°C.

(b) Grey tin stable *below* 13°C, white tin stable *above* 13°C.

trichloromethane This molecule is also known as *chloroform* and has been used as an anaesthetic. Trichloromethane is a substituted **alkane**. It is a colourless, volatile *liquid* which boils at 62°C. See **tetrachloromethane**.

triple bond Contains three shared pairs of **electrons** and is found in **alkynes** and **nitrogen**-containing **compounds**. Examples:

ethyne H—C≡C—H   nitrogen N≡N

tritium The **isotope** of **hydrogen** which contains two **neutrons** in the **atom**. Tritium is a **radioactive** gas.

UHT (ultra-heat treatment) A heat-treatment process to reduce the number of micro-organisms present in food in order to extend its shelf-life. UHT milk is heated to 140 °C for between 2 and 4 seconds and then cooled rapidly to 20 °C. If it is packed under sterile conditions and unopened, UHT milk can be kept at **room temperature** for up to 5 months. See **pasteurization, sterilization**.

ultra-violet radiation (u.v.) Invisible radiation which has a slightly higher frequency (energy) than violet light. It is produced in large amounts by stars, e.g. the sun. The radiation in large amounts is harmful to humans — skin cancers can result. Not much of the u.v. radiation from the sun reaches the earth. Much of it is filtered out by the **ozone layer** in the stratosphere. See **Earth's atmosphere**.

units Fixed quantities which are used as standards to measure other things. See **SI units**.

Measurement	Unit
Distance	Metre (m)
Time	Second (s)
Mass	Kilogramme (kg)

universal indicator A mixture of indicators. Because it is a **mixture** it changes colour several times as the **pH** of the **solution** changes. It is possible to tell the approximate pH of a solution by adding a few drops of universal indicator to it and reading the pH off the chart such as the one shown below. Universal indicator paper strips are also available

Colour	←red orange yellow green blue purple→													
pH	0 1 2 3 4 5 6 7 8 9 10 11 12 13 14													

unleaded petrol **Petrol** which does not contain the **fuel** additive tetraethyl lead. Instead, **methanol** (5%) and its derivative, methyl tertiary butyl ether (MTBE) (15%), are used. Unleaded fuel does not give rise to lead **pollution**. See **octane rating**.

unsaturated compounds Carbon compounds which possess double or triple bonds between two **carbon** atoms are said to be unsaturated.

They contain more electrons in their bond than a normal single bond. Because of this they are reactive. They tend to react through addition reactions forming new bonds with the electrons they possess, e.g. alkenes become alkanes.

uranium A metallic **element** which has three naturally occurring **isotopes** (masses 234 —

(a)

$$\overset{\diagdown}{\underset{\diagup}{C}} = \overset{\diagdown}{\underset{\diagup}{C}}$$

alkenes

$$- C \equiv C -$$

alkynes

(b)

ethene (unsaturated) $\xrightarrow{H_2}$ ethane (saturated)

unsaturated compounds (a) Common examples of unsaturated compounds, (b) addition reactions form new bonds.

trace, 235 − 0.7%, 238 − 99.3%). They are all radioactive and eventually decay to give stable isotopes of **lead**.

238.1

92 | U | 19.0

1133 | 3930

uranium

Uranium is used as a **fuel** in nuclear power stations. In some types of reactor, uranium oxide

U_3O_8 is used. In others uranium containing a higher proportion of U-235 is used (enriched uranium). In the fast-breeder reactor uranium 238 is turned into **plutonium** 239 which can then be used as a fuel. See **nuclear reaction**.

urea A colourless substance found in the urine of all mammals, but also produced commercially by the reaction of **carbon dioxide** and **ammonia** at 200°C and 400 atmospheres pressure.

$$CO_2(g) + 2NH_3(g) \rightarrow NH_2CONH_2(g) + H_2O(g)$$

Urea is used as a **fertilizer**, in the production of **adhesives** and pharmaceuticals and in the production of **urea/methanal resins**.

urea

urea/methanal resin A **condensation polymer** formed by the reaction of **urea**, NH_2CONH_2, and **methanal**, HCHO. It is used as an **adhesive** (e.g. in the production of **chipboard**) and in the production of electrical plugs and sockets. See **melamine**.

urethanes **Monomers** for the production of

polyurethanes which are important in the making of **synthetic foam**.

vacuum A space where there are no **atoms** or **molecules** present. It is impossible to obtain a *perfect* vacuum but we talk of a *partial* vacuum when the **pressure** is extremely low. The pressure is low outside the **Earth's atmosphere**, in space, and this is usually thought of as a vacuum.

valency A *combining power*, i.e. the usual number of **bonds** which an **atom** forms when making **compounds**. More precisely, the valency of an **element** is the number of **electrons** that it needs to form a compound or **radical**. The electrons can be *given to* another element; they can be *taken from* an element; they can be *shared*.

Some elements always have the same valency, e.g. **hydrogen** = 1, **oxygen** = 2 (except in **peroxides**), **sodium** = 1, **magnesium** = 2. For example,

(a) Sodium has a valency of 1. Sodium gives one electron away when it forms the sodium ion Na^+, e.g. NaCl.

(b) Oxygen has a valency of 2. Oxygen accepts two electrons when it forms the oxide ion O^{2-} or it forms covalent compounds, e.g. SO_2, CO_2, N_2O.

(c) Hydrogen and bromine have valency of 1. They both give one electron to make the

H−Br **covalent bond** when they form hydrogen bromide.

Transition elements however have more than one valency: **iron** = 2,3; **cobalt** = 2,3; **copper** = 1,2. The valencies of some common elements and ions are shown in the following tables:

+1		+2		+3	
Lithium	Li^+	Calcium	Ca^{2+}	Aluminium	Al^{3+}
Sodium	Na^+	Magnesium	Mg^{2+}	Iron(III)	Fe^{3+}
Potassium	K^+	Zinc	Zn^{2+}		
Silver	Ag^+	Iron(II)	Fe^{2+}		
Ammonium	NH_4^+	Lead	Pb^{2+}		

−1		−2		−3	
Fluoride	F^-	Sulphide	S^{2-}	Phosphate	PO_4^{3-}
Chloride	Cl^-	Oxide	O^{2-}		
Bromide	Br^-	Carbonate	CO_3^{2-}		
Iodide	I^-	Sulphate	SO_4^{2-}		

vanadium   A **transition metal**. Its chief use is in the production of vanadium-steel **alloys** which are valuable because of their high tensile strength and hardness, that is, their ability to withstand stress. They often include **chromium** or **manganese** in addition to vanadium.

Vanadium(v) oxide V_2O_5 is the **catalyst** used in the **contact process**.

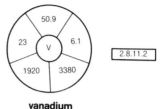

vanadium

Van der Waals' forces (or **Loudon forces**) Weak forces between **atoms**. They are caused by the movement of **electrons** within the atoms. **Elements** which only have these forces to hold them together, e.g. the **noble** gases, have very *low* **melting** and **boiling points**.

vapour Atoms or **molecules** in the gaseous state *but* below their *critical temperature*, i.e. the **temperature** above which **liquid** cannot exist.

For example, when water evaporates from a saucer when it is left in the house, *water vapour* is formed and not **steam**.

veneer A very thin sheet of wood, cut from a log. Veneers from attractive woods such as mahogany, walnut, oak and yew are used as coverings for cheaper materials to give them an improved appearance.

vinegar A **solution** which is made by the action of bacteria on wine or cider. It contains about 4% **ethanoic acid**. It is used widely in the food industry for preserving foods.

vitamins Chemicals which are important to the proper working of the body. They tend to be complex **organic** molecules which cannot be made in the body but which must be eaten, as in dairy products (vitamin A) or fruit (vitamin C).

volatile Easily turned into a **vapour**. Such substances either have **boiling points** which are near **room temperature**, e.g. **ether** or propanone; or they are **solids** which **sublime**, e.g. **carbon dioxide**. **Liquids** which are volatile *and* flammable (see **flame**) are very dangerous because of the risk of **explosions**. Care has to be taken with their storage and handling. **Petrol** is such a liquid.

volume The amount of space a substance occupies. **Solids** and **liquids** have fixed volumes but a **gas** will have the same volume as the container it occupies. The larger the container is, the *lower* is the **pressure**. The volume of a gas can easily be changed by compressing it but it is much more difficult to change the volumes of solids and liquids. *Hydraulic* brakes in a car depend on this property of a liquid. Volumes are measured in cubic centimetres (**cm**^{3}).

volumetric analysis A method of **quantitative analysis** which uses accurately measured volumes of **solutions**. See **titration**, **burette**, **pipette**.

vulcanization The process of adding **sulphur** to **rubber** to make it harder. See **cross-linking**.

washing soda Hydrated sodium carbonate ($Na_2CO_3.10H_2O$). The name comes from the use of the salt to soften water which was to be used for washing. See **hardness of water**.

water (H_2O) an **oxide** of **hydrogen**:

$$2H_2(g) + O_2(g) \rightarrow 2H_2O(l)$$

It is one of the most common **compounds** on Earth. It is the best known **solvent** and is needed by all living things.

Water is a colourless **liquid** and some of its more important properties are shown here:

(a) It has a freezing point of 0 °C.
(b) It has a boiling point of 100 °C.
(c) It has a density of 1.0 g/cm³ (water has a maximum density at 4 °C).

Unusually, water expands on solidification. This accounts for ice floating and water pipes bursting. It does not conduct electricity although it can be electrolysed if small amounts of **acid**

(H_2SO_4) or **alkali** (NaOH) are added. The products are **hydrogen** and **oxygen**:

$$2H_2O(l) \rightarrow 2H_2(g) + O_2(g)$$

A test for the presence of water is by changing the colour of **anhydrous salts**:

$$CuSO_4(s) + 5H_2O \rightarrow CuSO_4.5H_2O(s)$$
white   blue

These tests show that water is present and not that the water is **pure**. To show purity, the **boiling point** of the liquid could be taken.

Water is found in the **atmosphere**, in lakes, rivers, glaciers and the oceans. It is found in rocks and in living creatures. Water is continually moving from place to place on the Earth (see the **water cycle**).

The most important chemical property of water is its use as a **solvent**. Water has **polar bonds** and so can dissolve ionic solids such as sodium chloride (NaCl) as well as polar solids such as **glucose** ($C_6H_{12}O_6$).

The water which we drink is never pure. It always contains small amounts of **gas** (e.g. **oxygen** and **carbon dioxide**) and, depending on the source of the water, **solids** are dissolved in it too, some of which make the water hard. See **hardness of water**.

water cycle The continual movement of **water** around the Earth, both in the oceans and in the **air**. Water falls to Earth as rain, snow, hail, sleet, and freezes out of the air as frost and **ice**. It falls onto the oceans and these act as a vast source of water. It falls on land and here it enters the Earth and eventually flows into lakes and rivers and then flows into the oceans. From these large areas of water, **evaporation** occurs and water re-enters the **atmosphere**. In this way the cycle continues. Plants and animals take water out of the ground for their own use and it can re-enter the atmosphere (transpiration, excretion and **respiration**) or the Earth. Large quantities of water are stored as glaciers and the polar ice caps. See diagram overleaf.

water of crystallization **Water** which is chemically bonded within **crystals**. Examples are:

$$CuSO_4.5H_2O \qquad Na_2CO_3.10H_2O \qquad CaSO_4.2H_2O$$

Water can be removed by heating, leaving the **anhydrous** salt. This can happen because the chemical **bonds** are weak. Some **salts** which include water of crystallization lose some of the chemically bonded water simply on exposure to the air. This is called **efflorescence**.

weak acids and bases See **strengths of acids and bases**.

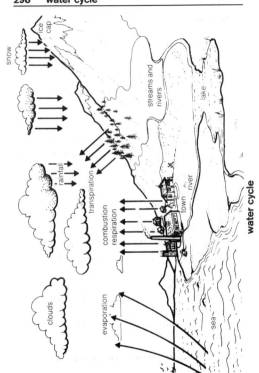

water cycle

whitewash   A **suspension** of calcium hydroxide in **water**. This is used as a temporary '**paint**' for things such as the white lines on hockey pitches. Exposure to **carbon dioxide** in the air, turns the slightly **soluble** hydroxide into the insoluble calcium carbonate:

$$Ca(OH)_2(aq) + CO_2(g) \rightarrow CaCO_3(s) + H_2O(g)$$

wool   A **natural fibre** which comes from sheep, goats and similar animals. Wool is a **protein** fibre which has a crinkled and scaly structure. Because of this, the fibres are elastic and can trap air. Clothes made from wool tend to be warm.

X-rays   Electromagnetic radiation which has high **energy**. It is produced by firing **electrons** at **metals**. It is a very penetrating radiation and will easily pass through flesh but is stopped by bone and other dense substances such as metals.

xenon   One of the few **noble gases** which have been found to form **compounds**. Even so, only the two most reactive elements, **flourine** and **oxygen**, have succeeded, e.g. XeF_2, XeF_4, XeF_6, XeO_3. The element is used to fill light bulbs and fluorescent tubes. See overleaf.

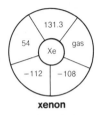

xenon

yeasts Microscopic organisms which are very useful to humans. They are used in baking and brewing. In brewing, they are used to convert **sugars** into **ethanol**:

$$C_6H_{12}O_6(aq) \xrightarrow{\text{yeast}} 2C_2H_5OH(aq) + 2CO_2(g)$$

glucose   ethanol   carbon dioxide

The results are alcoholic drinks such as beer and wine. The **carbon dioxide** is either collected and sold or it is allowed to escape into the atmosphere.

In baking, it is the carbon dioxide which is useful. The dough is mixed and then the **sugar** and yeast react in the dough to produce the **gas**. The gas makes the dough expand (rise) and the mixture becomes much lighter. Yeasts contain **enzymes** and it is these substances which act on the sugars. See **fermentation, zymase**.

yield of a reaction   Many chemical reactions do not produce as much product as would be expected from looking at the chemical equations. It is useful to express the amount of product as a percentage of what it is theoratically possible to produce:

$$\text{Yield of reaction} = \frac{\text{amount of product produced}}{\text{maximum amount of product that it is possible to produce}}$$

For example,

$$CuO(s) + H_2(g) \rightarrow Cu(s) + H_2O$$

copper(II) oxide   hydrogen   copper   water

80 g   → 64 g (maximum yeld)

If 80 g of oxide actually produce 56 g of copper metal the percentage yield of the reaction is $(^{56}/_{64} \times 100)\% = 87.5\%$.

Z   The symbol which is given to represent the **atomic number** of an **element**, i.e. the number of **protons** in the **atom**.

zinc   A **transition metal** which is found in the first transition series in the **periodic table**.

It is a dense grey metal which is reactive towards **acids** but which does not react with cold water. The metal is used in the **alloy, brass**, and also in the protection of **steel** by **galvanizing**. Zinc is extracted from the sulphide **ore** (ZnS).

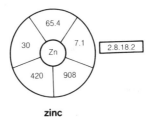

zinc

Zinc compounds

Zinc oxide ZnO	This has a use in medicine — zinc oxide cream. It is used as a protection against skin irritations, e.g. nappy rash. It is also used in paints. Zinc oxide and hydroxide are **amphoteric**.

zymase The enzyme present in **yeasts** which is responsible for the formation of **ethanol** and **carbon dioxide** from **sugars**.

APPENDIX A

A list of some useful common abbreviations and symbols you may encounter in scientific literature.

A   mass number; also Ampère — unit of electric current

aq   state symbol for aqueous solution usually as (aq)

A_r relative atomic mass

atm   atmosphere — a unit of pressure

α alpha Greek letter

β beta Greek letter

b.p.   boiling point

C   Celsius as in °C degree Celsius; also Coulomb — unit of electric charge (quantity of electricity)

cm^3 cubic centimetre, unit of volume

DC   direct current — the type of electricity produced from a battery

dm^3	cubic decimetre ≡ 1 litre, unit of volume
E	symbol for emf of a cell
e or e^-	electron
emf	electromotive force
g	gramme — unit of mass; state symbol for gas usually as (g); also acceleration due to gravity
H	enthalpy (ΔH = enthalpy change)
I	electric current
i.r.	infra-red radiation
J	Joule — unit of energy
k	prefix meaning 'one thousand times' i.e. kg = 1000 g
K	Kelvin —unit of temperature, $1\ K \equiv 1\ °C$
l	state symbol for liquid usually as (l)
m	mass; also metre — unit of length
M	molar — unit of concentration (molarity) e.g. 2 M

m^3	cubic metre — unit of volume
mol.	mole — unit of amount of substance
ml	millilitre, 1/1000 of 1 litre ≡ 1 cm^3
m.p.	melting point
M$_r$	relative molecular mass
n	neutron
N	Newton — unit of force
NTP	Normal temperature and pressure
p	proton; also pressure
P$_a$	Pascal — unit of pressure
p.d.	potential difference
pH	relates to a scale of acidity, e.g. pH = 1 very strongly acidic
Q	electric charge, quantity of electricity
s	state symbol for solid usually as (s); also second — unit of time
STP	standard temperature and pressure

t   time

T   temperature

$T\frac{1}{2}$ or $t\frac{1}{2}$ half-life (of radioactive isotope)

u.v.   ultra-violet

V   volume; also electrical potential
          difference (p.d.); also volt — unit of p.d.

Z   atomic number

APPENDIX B

Some common hazard signs and their meanings.

 EXPLOSIVE — This substance may explode if ignited, heated, or exposed to friction or a sudden shock.

 OXIDIZING — This substance can cause fire when in contact with combustible material.

 HIGHLY FLAMMABLE — This substance may easily catch fire under normal laboratory conditions.

 CORROSIVE — This substance can destroy living tissue.

 IRRITANT — This substance causes irritation to living tissue, e.g. skin may become red or blistered after repeated contact.

 TOXIC — This substance is a serious health risk. Toxic effects may result from swallowing, inhalation or skin absorption.

HARMFUL —

This substance is less of a health risk than a TOXIC one but should still be handled with care. It may cause harm by swallowing, inhalation or skin absorption.

RADIOACTIVE —

This substance emits radioactivity and should be treated with extreme care.